P9-DBO-783

THE HIDDEN VALUE OF A MAN

Gary Smalley and John Trent, Ph.D.

THE HIDDEN VALUE OF A MAN

THE INCREDIBLE IMPACT
OF A MAN ON HIS FAMILY

PUBLISHING

Colorado Springs, Colorado

THE HIDDEN VALUE OF A MAN
copyright © 1992 by Gary Smalley and John Trent, Ph.D.

Library of Congress Cataloging-in-Publication Data
Smalley, Gary,
    The hidden value of a man: the incredible impact of a man on his family / Gary Smalley and John Trent.
      p. cm.
    ISBN 1-56179-122-9 (hard)
    1. Man — United States — Psychology. 2. Communication in marriage — United States. 3.
    Communication in the family — United States. 4. Sex role — United States. I. Trent, John T. II Title.
    HQ1090.3.562 1992
    305.32—dc20

                                  92-18739
                                       CIP

Published by Focus on the Family Publishing, Colorado Springs, Colorado 80995.

Distributed by Word Books, Dallas, Texas.

Unless otherwise noted, Scripture quotations are from the Holy Bible, New International Version,
copyright © 1973, 1978, 1984 by the International Bible Society. Quotations identified as NASB are
from the *New American Standard Bible*, © 1960, 1963, 1968, 1971, 1972, 1973, 1975, and 1977 by
The Lockman Foundation.

People's names and certain details of case studies mentioned in this book have been changed to
protect the privacy of the individuals involved. However, the authors have attempted to convey the
essence of the experience and the underlying principles as accurately as possible.

Editor: Larry K. Weeden
Designer: Jeff Stoddard
Photographer: Rick Mueller

Printed in the United States of America
  93 94 95 96 97/10 9 8 7 6 5 4

To Gary and Norma's newly wed children:
Kari, who became Mrs. Roger Gibson on March 21, 1992; and
Greg, who married Erin Murphy on May 30, 1992.
May the Lord keep them faithful and loving as a
heritage to their own children.

TABLE OF CONTENTS

THE HIDDEN VALUE OF A MAN

CHAPTER 1

THE HIDDEN
VALUE OF A MAN

For the past several years, we've been sensing a strange uneasiness among men everywhere. What we see happening is much like what we witnessed recently during Operations Desert Shield and Desert Storm.

When the buildup of troops began and then the bullets started flying, our country saw an incredible happening on the home front. It was as if pent-up patriotism had been held in check so long that the conflict caused an explosion of flags, bumper stickers, parades, and speeches all saying, "We're proud of our men and women overseas, and we're proud to be Americans again."

It seemed as if the nation was waiting for something, some time, when the wounds of the Vietnam War could be healed and our country brought back together. And that's just what happened. In hundreds of cities small and large, parade routes were lined with cheering people welcoming home the troops from Saudi Arabia. But the Vietnam vets marching by got the loudest and the longest (and much-deserved) rounds of applause.

In the same way, we've sensed a pent-up frustration on the part of men that has also turned into an explosion. We've worked with couples and families, men and women, for nearly a quarter of a century now. And *never* have we seen such a nationwide, major explosion as we're witnessing today.

It's as if men are awakening from their own personal Vietnam experience of having been browbeaten and ridiculed for just being men by the media and some in the women's movement. For nearly 40 years, men have been pictured

1

by cartoon characters and dinner speakers as dense, unromantic, uncommunicative, uncaring, and on and on. But today, all over the country, men are coming out of the woodwork to stand up and challenge that image.

This other "Desert Storm" was largely ignored by the press, but it has moved man-to-man across the country, galvanizing men as we've never seen before.

For nearly 40 years, men have been pictured by cartoon characters and dinner speakers as dense, unromantic, uncommunicative, and uncaring.

A late-night call from a man in his fifties typifies what we're hearing everywhere we travel. His story, while admittedly picturing an extreme, captures the heart of this book. And it reminds us that a greater day is coming for the family.

We received the call not long ago, when we were live on a national, one-hour radio talk show. With only moments left in the program, the announcer said, "Let's try to squeeze in one more call."

The caller said, "Remember me, Gary? This is J.D."

J.D.? We were staring at each other with blank looks on our faces, at a loss to remember who J.D. was.

Then he said, "Gary, I'm the guy from Waco you talked to about his wife leaving him 13 years ago."

To be honest, the first thought that raced through my (Gary's) mind was, *Oh, no! We're going to finish this program with this man saying, 'All that advice you gave me never worked!'* But that's not what happened.

For a short time over the radio, and then in an extended conversation off the air, we got to hear the heartwarming story of a man who had incredible value and power in his home—just like every husband and father—yet never realized it until it was almost too late.

J.D.'s story was miraculous in another way as well. Many years ago, I (Gary) began my first book[1] by telling his story without knowing how it would end. But what he revealed that night on the phone was beyond what I'd hoped for or even thought possible. As we listened in joy and tears to "the rest of the story," we stared at each other and thought, *We're in the middle of writing this book, spending long hours trying to capture in the right words the most important principles we've ever shared with men. And suddenly here's J.D.'s story, almost a complete overview of our entire book!*

The lifelong damage J.D. had been doing to his wife and children had somehow escaped his attention. He often felt unneeded by them. But most of all, he was completely unaware that two tremendously powerful sources of strength were within him—both could build or weaken a loving home.

What happened to J.D. is one man's story, but it illustrates crucial issues all of us men need to look at. And it begins where I (Gary) first met him—at the end of the road.

JUST AN "AVERAGE" MAN

Like hundreds of men I've talked to since, J.D. had no idea an earthquake was coming. Sure, he had felt a few tremors and emotional aftershocks. But in his mind, his world seemed solid and secure.

At work, he was on the fast track: making decisions; moving up the ladder; having to get tough at times. That's the way he was at home, too: demanding; tough; insensitive; no different from most men on his block.

His wife would ask him to stop and pick up a can of coffee on his way home from work, and he'd thunder at her, "Why are you always running out of coffee!" He knew he wasn't the most sensitive person, but at least he was there! He was providing for her financially in a way he felt she ought to appreciate, and he figured that should more than make up for everything else.

He knew how to be strong. He knew how to "rule the roost." What he *didn't* know was that by failing to develop a side of himself that he rarely tapped into, he was setting himself up for a personal day of destruction.

Like many men, J.D. was blind to the pressures building in his wife—all under the surface—that finally blew up dramatically. Of all the things that have happened to him before or since, nothing shook every part of his world like the day she served him with divorce papers and ordered him to move out.

In that first marriage book I wrote, I told how J.D.'s experience pictured the end of the story for some men—a jolting wake-up call that brings his family life crashing down around him, and emotional aftershocks that affect his life, his health and business and what's left of his family, for years to come. But J.D. discovered something else that actually led to a new beginning—a way to build up his wife and guidelines that would restore his family and marriage—even his relationships at work—to a place he never thought possible.

What J.D. was to learn nearly 13 years ago and put into regular practice forms the basis of this book. What did he learn? The same types of things you'll discover:

- Why and how men become so powerful and valuable to their families
- How men are given two sources of power early in life, one more destructive than the other, but both with tremendous impact
- How to discover the secret to building a great sense of teamwork between husband and wife
- How to develop great friendships with other married couples that will "hold up our arms" during any times of marital difficulty
- How through just one phone call to a particular type of coach, we can join the ranks of the wise and see nearly instant improvement in our relationships
- How to find genuine, lasting motivation to do what we already know is right in our homes, and to follow through on those changes until success is reached
- How to overcome five major roadblocks to building solid relationships

We can hardly wait for you to finish this book and join with us and the thousands of other men around our country and beyond who are tired of the state of the family—men who yearn for a new day of strength for their marriages and families in the nineties and on into the twenty-first century.

J.D. is one of those thousands. And for him, "school" began at a sleepy, country courthouse in Waco, Texas. I went with him to the divorce proceedings, where his last ray of hope seemed to end.

HITTING BOTTOM ...
AND FINDING THE BOTTOM SOLID

"She's asking for too much money!" J.D. told me in shock. We were sitting on a well-worn wooden bench outside Courtroom C. As we talked, I realized the counsel I was giving him would have turned his lawyer's hair white.

We sat in the hall mulling over his soon-to-be ex-wife's monetary request as part of the divorce settlement. I knew his reaction wasn't based on finances. J.D. was on his way up the ladder toward the top of a large company and had far more than she was requesting in the bank. It was a question of control ... and of fighting to break the emotional stranglehold he had placed around her neck for years.

"That's not the issue," I told him. "You're going to get the money back anyway when you two get back together. So why not take this opportunity to show her you really value her and give her *double* what she's asking for!"

I'll never forget his look. "Double!" he growled.

It took J.D. 28 years to lose his wife. But once he put the principles he learned into practice, it took only 8 months to win her back.

I knew I was taking a risk. But I had also been counseling for years and had interviewed scores of men and women across the country who had been in J.D.'s shoes. And I knew this man's wife. His smothering, crippling, demeaning control had finally snuffed out any flame of feeling she had for him. But as yet, there wasn't another man who had lit a torch in her heart. It would take a lot of work to rekindle the dying embers, more work than he ever imagined. But he was desperate and willing to do anything it took to try to win her back.

J.D. had let her have it for 28 years. But now, in a monumental act of the will, he finally let her have her way for once ... and the money. In fact, he ended up giving her the entire checkbook that held their savings and saying, "Honey, you use this for you and the kids. I trust you. And I know you'll use it wisely." (To his amazement, she never took advantage of that generosity.)

A man who never, to his remembrance, cried in public stood with tears streaming down his face. All J.D. could do was watch as Judge Mormino lifted his gavel and pounded out the death sentence on a marriage J.D. had surely killed. *"Divorce granted."*

Before his wife walked out, J.D. had held all the power cards in their relationship: He called every game. Dealt out every decision. Changed any rule he wanted just so long as he won his way. But the day she quit playing the game and left, his life folded, too.

Suddenly he couldn't rely on his verbal strength to bully and control her.

He no longer had a voice in her life. And like an East Berliner, once she escaped from those walls of emotional bondage and first tasted freedom, she swore on her life that she would never be dominated by him again.

J.D. had hit rock bottom. But after the divorce, in those few breakfasts I had with him before we moved, I gave him a glimpse of a different kind of power. And when he joined with a small group in Waco (led by Ken Nair, a close friend, and Scott Baird, another close friend and one of our national board members today), he really came to understand this different type of power that can build up relationships instead of breaking them down. It can also open closed doors ... even padlocked ones.

It took J.D. 28 years to lose his wife. But once he put the principles he learned into practice, it took only 8 months to win her back. In front of the same judge, in the same courtroom where everything had ended, they were remarried and began life together again. And this time, they built a life worth living for both of them. In fact, their relationship became so strong that they stopped counting their wedding anniversaries from the first year they were married and started counting from the date of their remarriage.

For 12 years, J.D. loved and cared for his wife, drawing on a type of power he had never even considered before. They reunited on November 16, 1978. And by his account, they experienced more happiness and fulfillment than they ever thought possible until November 16, 1991, when at last she left his arms for the strong arms of her heavenly Father.

In this book, we want to introduce you to that rare type of value and power J.D. discovered. Not the kind of power that's normally found in the workshop or office, but a power every husband and father *already has* that is absolutely necessary if he's to win and hold the hearts of his loved ones. It's the kind of power that can turn around a broken home and family and, in time, a broken world.

For the many men whose relationships are far from being on the rocks, what you'll find here are clear charts pointing out the fast currents and hidden rocks in life's river, charts that can help to keep you and your family in safe waters.

You may not be a "reader"—many men aren't. But if you're a man, you need to read this book. For in it you'll gain a clear vision of how you can use your natural power for good. You'll also discover how to draw up a specific plan with your wife to raise your relationship with her to greater heights. Further, you'll come to understand why it's so difficult for most of us men to take on the task of building strong marriages and families, as well as how to overcome those mile-high roadblocks.

Every man has tremendous value. It's hidden at times, perhaps, but always there—a worth based on a type of power each man has within his grasp at home every day. In fact, during the writing of this book, we realized more completely just how influential the average man is. When you discover how to use this age-old power, you'll see a closeness and fulfillment in your marriage and family that you wouldn't have believed possible. And this power to build and bless others is captured in the reflection of a sword...

CHAPTER 2

THE TWO SWORDS OF VALUE IN EVERY MAN

These next two chapters may be difficult to read. They're filled with tough talk about subjects we men have to face. But we guarantee that if you'll make it through them, you'll then run into nearly nonstop encouragement that can help you take the high ground with your wife and family.

Why are two tough chapters necessary? Because without even realizing it, many of us are blasting away at our loved ones. We're turning ten-inch guns toward our wives and children and yanking the firing cord at close range. Why?

Because the average man fails to realize just how incredibly powerful his everyday actions and attitudes are—especially in the lives of those in his home.

Powerful?

Just how much power does the average man have today?

In our observation and counseling experience, many men today feel *powerless*, not powerful, especially when it comes to meaningful relationships. And that mind-set is weakening our homes and our nation, breeding irresponsibility at a breakneck pace, and increasing emotional pain in families tenfold.

In the pages that follow, we hope to show you that the average man has both great value and great power. More than he ever dreamed. He may not realize it. He may not understand it. He may not choose to believe it. But it's a power deep and wide and high enough to stagger the imagination.

It's the power to influence and change human lives.

It's a power in every home seen or unseen.

9

It's the power to send strong sons and clear-eyed, confident daughters into the world to right wrongs, fight worthy battles, and build strong families of their own.

It's a power that ripples outward for generations. Think of it! This power can positively affect our "children's children." What we do *today* in our homes can have a ripple effect on our great-great-grandchildren![1]

It can change a family tree forever.

In time, it can move a nation.

That's what it *could* do. But for so many men, men like J.D. ruling his home with an iron fist, that's not what's happening. Yes, the power is there. And yes, it's changing lives and affecting generations to come. But in many families, it's a power that destroys. And most men don't even realize that such power covers them like a five o'clock shadow.

WHEN CLARK KENT FORGOT HIS POWER

Imagine Clark Kent waking up one morning and somehow forgetting he possesses superhuman powers. He slaps the snooze button on his bedside clock radio and compresses it to the depth of an index card. At breakfast, he slams his coffee mug down on the table and sends it clean through two inches of splintered mahogany.

He yells his frustration at a sports article in the newspaper and cracks a thermal-pane window in the dining room. He also ruptures his wife, Lois's, left eardrum. She collapses in agony beneath the table as he heads back to the bathroom.

In the hallway, he brushes against Clark Junior, leaving him with a cracked collarbone and a severe concussion. On his way out the door, he swats the cat off his favorite chair and welds the unfortunate animal to the wallpaper. Leaving the house, he swings the door closed and rips it right off the hinges. He kicks a bicycle off the sidewalk, planting it 50 feet up in the neighbor's elm.

But that's unrealistic! How could Superman not realize his own powers? How could he miss seeing the devastation, pain, and havoc he has left in his wake? How could he look at the bruises, the tears, the brokenness, and the chaos and not realize he caused it all?

That's exactly the question we're asking in this book.

And how we answer it as men will not only shape our own families in the days ahead, but also our nation in the years to come.

How could men not realize how powerful they are? How could they fail to comprehend their vast and terrible ability to touch the lives of their families for good … or for unspeakable harm?

How, indeed. Ask any counselor: They see the results in the shattered lives of their clients. Ask any teacher: They see it in the vacant eyes of their students. Ask any employer: They find it in the chronic complaining and lack of motivation in their workers. And ask any pastor as he looks at the empty pews where men of God used to sit.

It has become almost an embarrassment to be a man today. And in the clamor for worldly power and prestige, most men are left feeling powerless, especially at home. Confused. Sitting on the sidelines when they need to be buckling their chin straps and getting into the contest.

Among a growing number of men we hear from today, there's a clear message that it's time we had a wake-up call ... before more wives provide an instant lesson in sensitivity by walking out, or children by rebelling. While the media have focused on every power group under the sun ("women's power," "black power," "gay power," "gray power," etc.), another kind of power is slipping off the back page and out of print. That's the power healthy manhood represents and always has. It's the power to shape souls and change lives for the better.

For some of us, it comes with a different look than we're used to, a different feel. But for all of us, it's a power that lies within our grasp. All we have to do is reach out and take hold of it.

Two Powerful Swords within Our Reach

Let us give you a picture of how valuable each man is. As a man, whether you realize it or not, you own two "swords," two forms of power. The handle of one gleams silver-blue, as though chiseled from a block of ice. You acquired the silver-handled sword early in your manhood, and you have continued to use it down through the years. You obtained it through sweat and grit and long, weary hours of labor. *It's the sword you use mainly in your job*, and it remains your constant sense of protection, an equalizer in a rough-and-tumble world. At times, its familiar weight makes it a cross between a security blanket and a lucky charm.

But you have a second sword as well. Its handle is burnished gold. This sword has been yours since birth, part of your inheritance, your birthright. You often leave it where it has been for as long as you can remember—mounted over the fireplace. Something ornamental. Something you may hardly notice. Something to dust twice a year. Exquisite, but men have been known to ask, "What's it good for?"

Most of the men you know in the work-a-day world want to wield the silver-handled sword. So do you. From the moment you completed your training in its use, it has been your deepest, most fervent desire to brandish that sword with all the strength, cunning, and endurance you can pull out of yourself. You read everything you can get your hands on about using it, and you endure endless days of study, disappointment, and heartbreaking toil; tense, sleepless nights; and frequent separations from your family.

For what purpose? To be regarded one day as a "Master of the Silver-Handled Sword." What else could a man desire?

It's time we had a wake-up call ... before more wives provide an instant lesson in sensitivity by walking out, or children by rebelling.

Yet, it's curious. The sword that looks so impressive among the sword handlers of the marketplace seems a heavy, awkward thing when you walk through your front door in the evening. It catches the screen door. The sheath seems to stick out and tear the wallpaper in the entryway. It has even knocked over the umbrella stand and a vase or two.

For that matter, you've found it extremely difficult to use the thing at home. You've tried to swing it around according to your training, but it causes your sons to wince and drives your daughters from your arms. Your faithful hound whines and slinks away when you pat the silver handle on your hip. At times, your family has even grown to despise it.

Many times, your wife wishes you would hang it on a peg outside the door and not bring it in the house at all. (Can you imagine?) Your oldest and closest friends grow cool and distant and lower their eyes when you draw it from its sheath and hold it to the light. And truthfully, the metal that gleams and flashes so brightly among your fellow sword handlers seems dull and commonplace in the firelight of home—more like tired, cold steel than the glinting, glimmering weapon you like to raise aloft in the village square. After all your polishing and sharpening and shining, within your own home it looks alarmingly like a too-large butter knife.

You stand by the hearth and contemplate these strange things when suddenly, you find yourself gazing at a reflection of firelight dancing in the molten gold of the "ornamental sword" hanging over the mantel. How it catches and holds the light! How it gathers the warmth of the room and reflects it back in greater glory!

Your own father rarely used it, just like his father before him. It may have been months since you've seen one used, even though you've heard strange rumblings of men beginning to openly carry it—even talk extensively about it in front of other men. But in your corner of the world, few of the sword handlers in the marketplace even speak of it.

But how beautiful it is! Why hadn't you noticed it more often? On a whim, you unhook it from its mountings and draw the sword from its finely tooled sheath. Catching and holding the red flames of a cherrywood fire, it seems to glow with a life of its own. The warmth flows down your arm and courses through your body.

What if there was a tool, you wonder, *that could draw my sons and daughters to me rather than thrust them away? What if it could carry the warmth of hearth fires from room to room and bring gladness and laughter?*

What if that tool also served as a weapon strong enough to drive back the darkness, banish loneliness from beneath this roof, overwhelm harsh words, force back the fears of childhood, overcome bitterness, slay the insecurities of adolescence, and kindle courage and hope whenever it was raised?

The gold-handled sword gleams in your hand like sunshine gathered from a thousand summer mornings. *And what*, you ask yourself with a growing sense of awe, *if I'm holding such a tool in my very hands?*

You do hold such a tool. And you do have a chance to use it, as well as your silver sword, for either tremendous good or great evil. The two swords are your future!

TWO KINDS OF POWER

The silver-handled sword we write of is a man's *positional power*. That's the clout, control, prestige, and authority that come to a man because of where he works or what he does. It's his job title, his resumé, whether he works on the line or supervises from the catwalk. It's the number of academic degrees he has earned or the way other men respect the clear mark of a craftsman when he finishes a job.

Positional power shows up clearly on a corporate flow chart. It's whom you know, whom you lunch with, where you've been, what you drive, and how many people report to you. It's the name on the door, the label inside your suit coat, the right to drive the company car, the title on your business card, or the key to the executive washroom.

As men, we're used to using this sword—and having it used against us. Books on positional power like *Dress for Success, Your Perfect Right, Power Negotiating,* and *How to Get Yours* fill the business section of most major bookstores.

Positional power centers on an image ... and doing whatever it takes, to whomever, to increase and maintain that image of excellence.

Personal power, on the other hand—the gold-handled sword—may or may not be accompanied by an impressive title, gold American Express card, or Ph.D. It's the ability to develop meaningful, fulfilling relationships; a willingness to do whatever it takes to strengthen our families and find the help we need to overcome any strains in our marriages.

An important aspect of personal power is our inner character, *who* we are. Words like warmth, sensitivity, dependability, determination, genuine compassion, affection, and caring all reflect a man's strength and value.

Read the following three paragraphs carefully. They begin to uncover the hidden value of a man.

It's as if our wives and children each have seven emotional and physical gas tanks inside them. These tanks need regular filling if our loved ones are to be normal and healthy. We have the power and opportunity to fill these tanks. This is our gold sword.

For example, they each have a touch tank that we help fill with hugs, holding hands, and so on. They also have a treasure tank, and our high-octane communication gas is essential for their survival.

It's true that everyone in a family helps to fill all seven tanks, but researchers are finding that the most-vital "gas" comes from the husband and father. We'll cover these crucial areas much more thoroughly and explain what a man can do so he can actually see and feel this healthy power in chapters 4, 5, and 6.

A short time ago, in a late-night conversation, I (John) encountered a striking illustration of the difference between positional and personal power. It's a picture that has haunted my thoughts ever since.

POWERFUL ... AND POWERLESS

"John," a friend named Ty told me, "you just can't imagine the feeling. Flying an F-16 is the closest thing you can get to being strapped onto a guided missile."

I believed him. We were drinking stale, inky coffee at some all-night pancake house with orange vinyl booths. It was very late, well after our twenty-year high school reunion had broken up. Several other groups were out barhopping. Ty and I, old football teammates, had drifted to the first open coffee shop we'd found.

Ty wanted to talk, and I was willing to listen in spite of the late hour and bad coffee.

The feeling my old high school buddy was talking about might have been the thrust and the G's of screaming over a blurred landscape at Mach 1. But knowing Ty, I felt sure the rush he described came from experiencing the indescribable sense of power.

What better picture of positional power? Your "position" is commanding the cockpit of one of the most formidable weapons ever designed. At your fingertips rests the capacity to hurl death, fire, and destruction at targets far beyond your range of vision.

For Ty, it was more than playing "Top Gun" in a variety of training exercises. He was the flight leader of an Air Force quick-deployment fighter group, the leading edge of the awesome American military machine. And that power was poured out in full measure in Operation Desert Storm as he and his squadron rained fire and brimstone on Saddam Hussein's capital, forcing the massive Iraqi armies out of Kuwait.

Ty had been the lightning of Desert Storm. And he loved it.

Even before his training, all through the years at the Academy, his vision was filled with fighter planes. He endured the pressure, the hazing, and the harassment of upper classmen, knowing that if he stuck with the program, some day he would have his very own "sword."

Now a veteran pilot and a still-youthful Air Force major, he had all the positional power a man could ask for. He was an expert in using the silver sword—respected by those ranking above him, saluted by everyone under him, counted on by those who flew with him, and admired by a rising generation of young air warriors.

He was also losing his family.

The breakup was imminent. By the time he got home, it might have already happened.

As we talked into the night in the corner booth, all the pride, swagger, and spit and polish began to melt away. The fun of screaming through the stratosphere wasn't such a big deal anymore. All his training as an elite Air Force officer gave him the confidence that he could walk away from any battle. But it never prepared him for the quiet warfare on the home front. And now his personal world was going up in flames.

My friend's eyes reflected pain, loss, and helpless frustration. For all his accomplishments and admirable positional power, Ty was a broken, lonely man. He had used his silver sword to win a war, but that same power had destroyed his family.

I have a mental picture of Ty that has hung in the back of my mind since I prayed for him and we parted company that night. I see him pulling his six-foot-two-inch frame out of the cockpit as a setting sun washes him with a scarlet sheen. I picture him walking slowly across the tarmac, a lonely figure whose eyes are hidden behind his metal sunglasses, carrying his helmet under his arm. And his ever present silver sword is buckled to his gray-green flight suit.

I can almost hear him thinking, *How could I be so powerful ... and yet so utterly powerless when I walk through my own front door? I'm an Air Force officer. A commander. Men salute me. Strapped in my war bird, I have the strength to smash a column of tanks. To sink a battleship. To level a city. Yet my own family is slipping through my fingers, and I can't do a thing about it.*

It's been more than 20 years since we played our last football game, but Ty has never really come off the field. He spent 20 years carefully squeezing out, bottling up, and protecting every measure of positional power from each competitive duty assignment. Two decades of flying high. And no doubt about it, he's made the grade, accomplished great things, even put his life on the line for his country.

There's great honor in serving our country and no shame in what he has won by his dedicated effort. But what he felt ashamed about was what he'd lost in collecting all his trophies. In all those years, all those days and hours, all that practice at using the silver sword, Ty seldom gave thought to his personal power ... until now.

He remembered ruefully all the times he openly resented being at home instead of hanging out at the air base. All those broken promises of weekend trips and romantic dinners. All that potential for good, for love, for memories that could have warmed the hearts of his children over the years. Without my having to say a word, he knew he had lived only half a life. For he had seen the gold sword used by other men in his squadron.

Three of the men he flew with were also great pilots, but they had great families as well. They had the kind of homes he dreamed of having and a skill with the gold sword that he now knew he needed—but time was running out.

In his own living room, all the military might in his grasp counted for nothing. He had his ribbons brought home from battle, but they garnered only a casual glance. He was a living "Top Gun." Yet after reaching the top, he would have gladly traded places with the lowliest, wingless airman if he could just have the affection, admiration, companionship, and love of his wife and children.

SECRET STRENGTH

We have another friend who, like Ty, wears a uniform. And his is an occupation that demands just as much skill at handling the silver sword. But there's one big difference. This man is a master at using *both* swords.

My (Gary's) nephew Bob is a paramedic who for years ran life-and-death calls in Watts, a rundown part of Los Angeles. Anyone old enough to remember the sweltering summer of 1965 remembers the riots that took place in Watts. Burning buildings. Bullet-ridden storefronts. And anyone who travels there today can still find times when it's more like a war zone than a neighborhood.

Many times Bob was called to the scene of a shooting, only to find himself and his partner coming under fire. He has been swung at, spit at, and cussed at ... by people whose lives he was trying to save! His line of work is a breeding ground for mistrust, cynicism, and apathy. You see so much pain, so much inhumanity, so many people who just stand by and do nothing that your view of humanity can barely rise above the gutter.

As jobs go, it's a great way to become as hard and calloused as the blacktop they race across to try to save lives. But while Bob could have focused only on his silver sword to try to cope, he chose to do more. That's why his ability to use the gold sword in the midst of all that hate and hostility has set him apart, like a rose growing up through the concrete.

As everyday observers of the great drama of life and death, paramedics as a group get very good at burying emotions ... and having them resurface later in a negative way. But when the pressures built up between a driver and his fellow paramedic, when a new widow had to be talked to, when a young person needed comfort, Bob was always called on. Why? Because he always has a listening ear, a bit of God's wisdom to share, and a standard of confidentiality that relieves fear and the burden of a person's heart.

Bob isn't a trained counselor. It just seems that way. He has a genuine love for people, even hard-to-love people, that draws others like a magnet.

When it comes to using the silver sword, any number of paramedics can show a person the ropes of the job. But when the foundations of their lives or careers are shaking, they suddenly remember a master of the gold sword, a man of seamless integrity and a warm, encouraging, accepting manner who has earned their admiration.

Just how respected is he in that world of silver swords? Has anyone really noticed that he can relate, comfort, and listen to others in an honoring way while being one of the very best at one of the hardest jobs in the world?

The answer is yes. I had the high honor of being at Bob's commissioning ceremony a year ago. He had been selected as one of only four paramedics in the entire Los Angeles Fire Department to be designated as departmental chaplains. No seminary degree. No Greek or Hebrew. But a godly love for others in the heat of battle that makes him a soldier's chaplain, someone in the trenches with

We're in a raging battle for the hearts of our families that begins at the cradle and never ends this side of the grave.

them whom they love and respect.

What happens when he goes home at night? His abilities with the gold-handled sword have made him just as much a hero to his wife. Nothing flashy. Just consistent love and unwavering commitment. And his wife reflects that love. She openly cares about *him*, not how high he's risen in the department.

Is it a matter of choosing between the two swords? Does it have to be one or the other?

Not at all. What we're talking about is a working knowledge of *both* positional and personal power. There are times when you'll have to be skillful with the silver sword in our work-a-day, competitive, difficult world. There were times when Jesus picked up the silver sword of His positional power: stilling the storm, casting out demons, and raising the dead. But more often than not, you'd see Him choosing the gold sword—His personal power expressed in touching a leper, calling a Zacchaeus to come down from a tree, and weeping unashamedly at the death of a friend.

There's great benefit in having two swords. But so many men have focused for so long on the silver-handled sword that they've neglected the deeper, stronger, longer-lasting power of the gold sword.

And that's what this book is about. We're calling men to pick up both weapons of warfare, for we're in a raging battle for the hearts of our families that begins at the cradle and never ends this side of the grave.

But can it really be done? *Can a man really learn to be an expert with two weapons at once?* The answer is, *he has to.* He has no choice—that is, if he wants to win the love of a child, the genuine affection of a wife, and a "Well done" from his God.

The pages that follow are actually lessons in swordsmanship. Many authors have written to help a man bear his silver sword with more skill, precision, or even brutality in the workplace. You can *Swim with the Sharks* while you learn *What They Don't Teach You at Harvard Business School* and master the *Leadership Secrets of Attila the Hun.* But we want to encourage you in the fine art of mastering your gold sword ... and seeing your relationships improve greatly as a result.

The price is high, but the rewards are immeasurable. And most of all, *it can be done.* It must be done. We're looking for a few good men. Men with no more education or will power than the average Joe. Men who make mistakes but are willing to humble themselves and get back in the fight.

Many of us are accustomed to picking up the gold sword. We already carry it openly and have used it to bless, encourage, and protect our families. For such men, the lessons of this book can help to sharpen the blade or narrow the point of a sword that is already in use. For others, however, these will be first lessons in what is truly a manly art.

And what will we be able to do once we master both swords? Get a raise at work? Make it to the top of our service clubs? Be prepared for political office?

Actually, we'll be more who we're called to be. More valuable as men. More capable of loving and leading others. Less lonely and isolated than we've ever been. And in the lives of our loved ones, we'll leave an emotional inheritance that can comfort them through each new season of life.

Are men really that valuable? Listen to what a friend named Roberta recently told us about her father's mastery of both swords during her early childhood and how that skill left her a legacy of love she has remembered all her life.

A CALLING WITHIN OUR REACH

Roberta's father was a cop who worked the graveyard shift in a rough Texas border town. Before he got that job, he had worked as a roughneck in the oil fields as a teenager, lived through ten months in Korea as a leatherneck, receiving two Purple Hearts, and served a short stint as an MP. He was a man's man who had put in time sharpening his silver sword.

He knew how to be strong when strength was needed. But he also understood the importance of picking up a gold sword, and he knew when the strongest thing he could give a child was softness.

As Roberta described it, one of her earliest memories was the paralyzing fear of losing her daddy. He was not only her father, but often he was her playmate as well. And always, he was her friend, her listener and encourager. Without fail, she could count on his eyes tearing up every time she stood to sing with the children's choir at church, and he never once walked out the front door without saying, "Remember I love you, honey."

What frightened her was the reality that in his line of work, some daddies never walked back in the door. Egged on by cruel neighborhood children who teased her with stories of police officers killed in the line of duty, her mind daily constructed its own horror story.

When you speak of a man's personal power, you immediately think of words reflecting character like warmth, sensitivity, dependability, determination, genuine compassion, *and* caring.

She painted the picture so well: a kindergarten girl in her nightgown, standing at the door of her parents' bedroom, watching as Dad knotted his tie, buttoned his uniform coat, and pulled on his shiny black boots to head out the door. No matter what she said or how hard she cried, she couldn't keep him from leaving.

Like a real-life scene out of *High Noon*, she couldn't stop him from walking into enemy territory, where the enemy didn't play by the rules. And then she would go to bed in a room full of nightmares that all her prayers couldn't seem to stop.

Roberta described his leaving for work as a deep fear, a vast, lingering terror she couldn't overcome ... until her father picked up his gold sword.

A man who knew only the silver-handled sword might have strapped on his gun, given his little daughter a peck on the cheek, laughed at her fears, and climbed into his squad car. But not this dad. He knew of a gold sword that over time could chase the fear out of a girl's heart.

Sitting in a big, overstuffed chair in the living room, he would let her crawl up into his lap for a bedtime story each night before he left for work. And though there were plenty of children's books in the house, she would always pick out the same one. It was only a tired story of a flop-eared dog named Ginger, but it held powerful images for her. Ginger, it seems, was a happy, carefree pup with a loving master and a fine, big yard to play in. Everything was wonderful in Ginger's little world until she wandered too far from home one day and got herself lost. Frightened and alone, the dog wondered if she would ever find her family again.

At this point in the story, Roberta would begin to cry. It seemed to happen every night. And every time, her father would gently hug her, *flip to the end of the book*, and show her that the story turned out all right. Ginger found her family. And then the tears would stop, because the little dog was finally home again.

"At the time," Roberta told us, "I remember how important it was for my father to read me that story. He must have understood it had a deep meaning for me, too. For months, I never remember him acting bored or asking me to pick out another story.

"I'm 48 years old, and it's just beginning to dawn on me how much my father blessed me by reading me that story time and again. Because each night, by his turning past the scary part and showing me the end of the book, he was showing me that everything would be all right in the morning. I'd wake up with my family and have my father's strong arms to hug me again, and I wouldn't have a care in the world.

"I can't think of a better gift a father could give his little girl than the loving security he poured into my life every night."

That's because his willingness to carry the gold sword gave him tremendous power and value in his home.

It is personal power.

It's power under control.

It's often referred to as love.

The silver sword and the gold sword, wielded by a man of faith. Tough assignment? You bet. But at least you're not alone. We're in training with you. And in every city we visit across the United States and beyond, men are joining us—men tired of winning at the games played at work and losing at the more important game of life at home.

It's never too late to begin a change process that can reverse generations of emotional damage. And even though we often feel powerless, we're actually

21

men of great power. We all have two major options, two swords we can put in our hands.

But what happens if, in spite of all this, we decide to pick up only one sword, the silver one, most of the time?

What damage do we really *do if we ignore the gold sword too often?* We are continually amazed at how powerfully men affect their loved ones. The next chapter can open your eyes even wider to the *negative* impact men can make.

CHAPTER 3

WHEN WE FAIL TO PICK UP THE GOLD SWORD

At this point you may be saying, "Come on! I'm not *that* powerful ... am I?" Well, let us show you in the next few pages how, if we ignore the warning signs all around us, we can greatly weaken our families, our churches, and eventually our nation.

What difference can it make when men misuse their power? Many men are affecting their families somewhat like the way a group of men greatly affected thousands of people by ignoring a warning and so producing a nightmarish Tuesday evening at New York's Kennedy International Airport.

Imagine that you're at the airport that evening with your family. It's the tail end of a brief vacation in New York City, and frankly, it feels like it. ("Whose idea was this, anyway?" you hear everyone muttering.)

After trudging for miles through the narrow canyons of Manhattan, bumping through countless stores, and enduring more numbing miles in taxis and tour buses on traffic-choked streets, you want nothing more than to stow your little tribe on the plane and leave the Big Apple far, far behind.

At last you're at the airport ... and about to run into something you never could have imagined.

Just as you're beginning to anticipate strapping yourself in and sipping that first Diet Coke, your eyes widen in disbelief as the "Flight Delayed" message flashes on the monitor at your gate. It can't be! Looking around, you notice that the same message is flashing on monitors at every gate! Something is shutting down the entire airport! And it will stay shut down for eight unbelievably long hours.

It's September 17, 1991, and you and multiplied thousands of other travelers have been stranded by one of the largest electronic communications breakdowns in national history.

Executives at telephone giant AT&T had a lot of explaining to do. It didn't get any easier when they discovered the massive shutdown could not be traced to any fire, accident, natural disaster, or equipment failure. It wasn't a case of some high-tech glitch or computer hiccup. What caused such a catastrophe? Try one simple word—negligence!

It turned out that employees at one of New York's main switching centers deliberately ignored several different alarm systems warning of impending overload. In spite of flashing red lights and audible warning signals, those men chose to shrug their shoulders and totally disregard the systems designed to avert that very disaster.

From wherever you're reading this book, ask yourself a crucial question: *Have you noticed any warning lights blinking in your home lately?*

RUNNING AWAY FROM REALITY

Deep down, men may realize something of the power they have to touch the lives of their wives and children. Yet many of us are like an absentminded Clark Kent. We're stumbling through our homes leaving sprung hinges, bone-deep wounds, splintered dreams, and shattered potential. We have no real concept of the damage caused by our actions, our words, our absence, even our silence. As with smoking or alcohol abuse, we don't see the damage immediately. So it's easy to think that because everything looks fine on the outside, problems aren't building up on the inside.

We can go for weeks acutely aware of our feelings of powerlessness, however, especially at home. And on those occasions when we do try to be powerful in our own way, it can often bring suspicion and rejection—especially from our wives. And that leads to further confusion about whether we really have any meaningful value and power.

Most of us men play hardball at work, where we feel we have the home-field advantage, and hard-to-get at home with our wives, where it seems we're on the visiting team's turf.

We somehow fail to realize that once we marry and become part of a family, whatever we do has life-shaping and, many times, irreparable implications. A man may try to deny until he's blue in the face that he even has a gold sword or that using it makes any real difference in his home.

He can't run away from his inherent power to influence those who depend on him, however. Why? On the pages that follow, we'll consider just a few reasons.

A CHILD'S HEART IS WITHIN A MAN'S REACH.

You don't have to be a pediatric heart surgeon to penetrate the chest cavity of a child. The heart of a little boy is already in his dad's hands. The heart of a little girl already lies exposed to her father's touch.

The heart is a delicate instrument. Don't be misled by wishful notions about "youthful resilience." ("Oh, go ahead and divorce. The kids will get over it.") Even the secular world is beginning to realize the lasting damage done to both children and adults by divorce.[1]

A child's heart is easily bruised. Easily torn. Easily broken. And once seriously damaged, no team of surgeons in God's world can repair it. Only the Almighty Himself has the skill to restore its original balance, potential, and capacities. And that may not happen this side of eternity. It's a sobering thing to hold a boy's or girl's heart in the cupped palm of your hand.

You've probably heard of senior military men who shake their heads and say, "Why in the world would our government build a $100 million tank equipped with unbelievably intricate electronic systems and a mind-staggering array of state-of-the-art weaponry and then put it in the hands of some 18-year-old kid?"

There's no good answer for that question. It's just the way things are, the way wars have always been fought. And why in the world would an all-knowing God allow a sensitive, fragile child's heart, with the potential for such incredible love, lifelong trust, and deep devotion, to be placed in the hands of powerful but often careless men—men who regularly fail even to see that a gold sword hangs within their reach?

There's no good answer for that question, either. But it's the way things are in this often-out-of-order world of ours.

How fragile is the heart you hold in your hands? What other instrument can be damaged for half a century or more by a single whispered sentence? What scientific, electronic equipment can be severely harmed by a single broken promise?

As we get into this chapter, we don't want you to feel the way we have sometimes when reading marriage or parenting books. At times we've felt guilty or hopeless because of all our own failures at home, and we don't want to be "beat over the head" by the author. So even if some of the stories here trigger shame, the remaining chapters can give you hope and encouragement.

Most children and wives long for us to pick up our gold swords at *any* age and begin to repair the relationship. We promise that if you'll keep reading, you'll see clearly how to design and use a gold sword. But first we have to face the reality of how powerful we are.

Recently, a 40-year-old man we counseled told us about a Saturday morning 28 years before that nearly stopped his heart—and is still affecting him today!

"I was just 12 when my Boy Scout troop planned a father-son camp-out," he said. "I was thrilled and could hardly wait to rush home and give my father all the information. I wanted so much to show him all I'd learned in scouting, and I was so proud when he said he'd go with me.

It's easy to think that because everything looks fine on the outside, problems aren't building up on the inside.

"The Friday of the camp-out finally came, and I had all my gear out on the porch, ready to stuff it in his car the moment he arrived. We were to meet at the local school at 5:00 P.M. and car pool to the campground. But Dad didn't get home until 7:00 P.M.

"I was frantic, but he explained how things had gone wrong at work and told me not to worry. We could still get up first thing in the morning and join the others. After all, we had a map. I was disappointed, of course, but decided to just make the best of it.

"First thing in the morning, I was up and had everything in his car while it was still getting light, all ready for us to catch up with my friends and their fathers at the campground. He had said we'd leave around 7:00, and I was ready a half hour before that. But he never got up until 9:30.

"When he saw me standing out front with the camping gear, he finally explained that he had a bad back and couldn't sleep on the ground. He hoped I'd understand and that I'd be a 'big boy' about it ... but could I please get my things out of his car, because he had several 'commitments' he had to keep.

"Just about the hardest thing I've ever done was to go to the car and take out my sleeping bag, cooking stove, pup tent, and supplies. And then—while I was putting my stuff away and he thought I was out of sight—I watched my father walk out to the garage, sling his golf clubs over his shoulder, throw them into the trunk, and drive away to keep his 'commitment.'

"That's when I realized my dad never meant to go with me to the camp-out. He just didn't have the guts to tell me."

How do you recalibrate a boy's heart after it has been damaged by a dad's broken promise?

How do you restore the capacity to trust after trust has been shattered?

How do you bring back a boy's joy and the sparkle in his eyes after they've been carelessly quenched?

That "boy" is now a man in counseling. His father is dead, but memories of a hurtful past have affected him and his own family *for years*. Is that not incredible power?

With God's help, a man can draw from the unfathomable depths of a child's heart the capacities to love, trust, serve, share, give, and create. Or he can twist it beyond repair so that it pumps out abuse, neglect, anger, and contempt—consequences that often last a lifetime.

We realize that some of the stories we tell in this book may seem like extremes of manly misconduct. In many cases, however, we've toned down the actual happenings! Thankfully, we realize many of you reading this book are not guilty of such offenses against your families. You may have the best intentions in the world, genuinely wanting what's best for your loved ones.

Yet even the finest intentions can lead to unwanted ends. Like the grown-up Peter Pan in the recent movie *Hook*, we men can easily get so wrapped up in our silver-sword careers that we lose sight of how our obsession with work affects our families. And since none of us can count on having a pirate come back from never-never land to force us to rethink our priorities, we hope to do the job in a slightly less confrontational way with this book!

We can hardly wait for you to read chapters 5 and 6, where you'll see how to create your own gold sword; and then for you to read chapters 12 and 13, where you'll see how joining with a group of men can help steady your arm as you hold that sword high in your home. That's vitally important, because no man can walk away from the fact that his child's heart lies within his hand. He will either damage it by using his silver sword too much or protect and nurture it by choosing to use his gold one.

THE POWER OF LIFE AND DEATH LIES WITHIN A MAN'S REACH.

Writer Gordon Dalbey describes a deeply moving church meeting where the congregation had just watched the powerful anti-abortion film *The Silent Scream*. Stung in heart and stirred to prayer, men and women began interceding for the pregnant young women faced with the appalling choice of bringing an unwanted baby to term or destroying it in the womb.

Others prayed for the parents of the young women, for the doctors and nurses in the abortion clinics, for the unborn babies themselves, and for the conscience of the nation.

Yet Dalbey felt a strange uneasiness. Something seemed missing somehow. Overlooked. "Lord, is there something else?" he asked.

"Almost at once the words burst forth in my mind: Pray for the men! No one is recognizing that without a man to impregnate the woman, the abortion issue would not exist."[2]

Can a fact become so obvious that we cease to recognize it? It's men who

The Bible has a word to describe "safe" sex: It's called marriage.

impregnate women! The ultimate "choice" in the issue belongs to the man. Even if she desired sexual intercourse, it would be very difficult for a woman to force herself on a man. It's a man's choice to plant his seed in the body of a woman and leave her with the heart-wrenching, life-blasting choices that often follow.

As we write this chapter, the lead story in the morning news is about Magic Johnson meeting with President Bush regarding AIDS education. Magic Johnson is HIV positive because of having engaged in "unsafe" sex, and his declaration of that fact has made him a hero, landed him an appointment to a presidential commission, and generated huge outpourings of support and adulation.

We hurt for his wife and soon-to-be-born child over what's coming. We grieve for the terrible consequences he faces and the loss of all his athletic talents and gifts. He is battling a killer no one has defeated, and his illness is terrible in every sense of the word. *But is he a hero?*

How does practicing "unsafe" sex with more than a thousand women make him admirable? He should be recognized for what he did on the basketball court, not for what he did or didn't do in a thousand bedrooms.

If he never once used a condom or other means of birth control, as he claims, where's the untold story? How many women became pregnant as a result of his choice to be promiscuous? How many of those women went on to have abortions ... or will go on to become HIV positive? In no way are we minimizing the tragedy, but we also don't feel we ought to glorify or even condone what led to the tragedy.

The Bible has a word to describe "safe sex": It's called *marriage.*

We've thrown God and public prayer out of our schools and put condoms in, and we actually wonder why we've got a generation of underachieving, rebellious, promiscuous children?

Abortion, like rape, is a man's issue. In this day of AIDS and quick-fix abortions, it's the power of life and death, and it's within a man's power to decide.

THE STRENGTH OF A FULFILLING MARRIAGE IS WITHIN A MAN'S REACH.

It takes two to participate in a great marriage. In chapter 9, we'll see just how dramatically a woman participates in either building a marriage or taking it apart brick by brick—often without even knowing why. But the biggest need we see today is to challenge men to use their power for good and to understand how that power affects their wives and children for years to come.

Just think about how much our friend Judy gave up the day she married Mark. Instantly, she gave up her maiden name at the altar. A few months later, she left her life-long place of residence to follow him to graduate school in another state. And for years, she postponed her own education so she could work and they could eat while he was in school.

She made sacrifice after sacrifice because she loved him. She trusted him. He had chosen her above all others, and he had stood right next to her, holding her hands, as he said those solemn words before God, her family, and many witnesses.

She added up the days until school would be over and better days would come. She banked on a future where he would give back to her, measure for measure, the love and concern she had lavished on him. But she never counted on him having an affair with another student his fourth year in graduate school and divorcing her within eight months of graduation.

Is it any wonder that many women are militant about what despicable creatures we men can be? Can you blame Judy for never wanting to trust another man and even questioning the love of her heavenly Father? Mark had moved her, sexually used her, denied her the opportunity for her own education, and then left her for a "prettier" woman—with the hearty agreement and admiration of his male friends! And it happens hundreds of times every year, all across our country.[3]

If a man doesn't think he's powerful, he should be forced to view a wide-screen movie of the aftermath of his leaving. The shock, anger, and devastation in his wife's eyes. The tears that fill his children's eyes when they find out Daddy isn't coming back. The confusion that surrounds them, the emptiness that crowds the dinner table, and the shame that settles like a cold dew on each one left behind. Even more, he should be somehow forced to *feel* the emotions of what he's done.

The greatest damage done to the little ones is that they can't seem to rid themselves of anger. That unresolved anger is what poisons their future, though it's not usually visible until they reach their twenties or thirties.

About a year ago, I (John) met with a man whose car was packed and ready to go. He "didn't want to leave," he said. "I really do love my family" were the words that came out of his mouth. Yet he was planning to unpack his suitcases in a rented apartment, not in the home he and his wife had so carefully picked out. He was confident that putting physical distance between him and his wife would somehow dissolve the emotional tensions between them; that leaving a wife and two preschool sons alone and heartbroken was for the best.

But *whose* best? Certainly not his family's, our country's, or this world's! He didn't stay around to see his wife struggle with the mower to try to keep the yard presentable. He offered no help when both kids went down with the chicken pox within two weeks of each other. He held out no hope of his coming back other than to sweep into the driveway unexpectedly for a few minutes now and then, always with presents for the boys that were nothing more than guilt offerings to relieve his nagging conscience and convince himself he was being a "responsible" parent.

Mark, and many like him, should be arrested. Like hit-and-run drivers, they've devastated lives by misusing their power and then deciding the solution to the problem was to leave the scene of the accident.

When will we men stop blaming or shaming? When will we realize that we have it in our power to build fulfilling marriages? We can get the help, face the demons, read the books, attend the support groups, and do whatever it takes to be healthy enough to present our wives as "holy and blameless" before the Lord.[4]

That Ephesians passage assumes a man is healthy when it says, "Husbands ought to love their wives as their own bodies.... After all, no one ever hated his own body, but he feeds and cares for it."[5]

But we meet with men constantly who aren't healthy. They neglect their wives, and they also destroy their own bodies with a combination of alcohol, drugs, anxiety, and/or illicit sex. Life-shortening addictions are a dime a dozen among men who fail to nurture their wives. And many of these men are simply reliving addictive patterns passed down by another group of men—their fathers (more on this in chap. 10).

For the first few years, a man might rationalize problems in his marriage as something wrong with his wife's past. But once four or five years have slipped by, we have to stop blaming the past. It's our responsibility as husbands to "present our wives" whole and complete, and if they aren't headed in the right direction, we're pointing them down the wrong road and need to admit to ourselves that we may require help in getting things turned in the right direction.

As men, the power to create a fulfilling marriage is within our reach. But not without sacrifice.

I (Gary) talked recently with a desperate man. His wife had just left him. His children were now miles away. There was even a court order against his visiting or talking with any of them.

"I want my family back! *I want my family back!*" he sobbed on the phone.

He wanted to fly out immediately and meet with me in Phoenix. However, the Scriptures give clear counsel when it comes to advising others. There we read, "Better a neighbor nearby than a brother far away."[6] Knowing I could be that "brother" who prayed for him at a distance but that he needed a "neighbor" close by to counsel him, I challenged him to find a local pastor or Christian therapist with an outstanding reputation.

"But I can't afford to go to counseling!" he said, suddenly losing all the emotion in his voice.

"Then sell one of your motorcycles and use that money," I told him.

"No way!" he said indignantly. "I'm not selling any of my stuff!"

And that was the problem. He could cry about ruining his relationship with his wife and children, but he wasn't willing to do enough to change. In his mind, the two dirt bikes in the garage were *necessities*. He was "powerless" to get counseling because he couldn't afford it. But what he really refused to pay for were the kind of personal changes that could have won his family back.

The choice is ours; we have the power to build fulfilling marriages. And that power doesn't stop at the door to our homes. Many men have taken their silver swords and built financial and industrial empires ... while others have used their power to drive a stake into the very heart of our nation.

THE DESTRUCTION OF OUR SOCIETY LIES WITHIN A MAN'S REACH.

There's no doubt that men, by God-given design, are leaders in science, industry, research, and religion. But that's not all they lead in. While they have a major role in building our society, they take an even greater lead in destroying it.

Look to our prisons, where 99 percent of those who sit on death row are men, and 95 percent of those who fill all the bunks are male.

Come upon the carnage caused by a drunken driver and you'll see the footprints of a man 91 percent of the time. Men are also responsible for 75 percent of all traffic accidents.

Thumb through 98 percent of the wanted posters for known drug dealers.

Look at those who profit the most from abortion clinics.

Uncover those who gladly serve as mercenaries for the mob or foreign governments.

Line up those who are responsible for more than 90 percent of child and spousal abuse cases.

Expose the billions of dollars spent by industry because of alcohol and drug abuse.

Turn to those who really hold the responsibility for teenage pregnancy, prostitution, and pornography.

Pause and look around, and you're looking at men, plain and simple.

When are we going to wake up to the fact that we, as men, are responsible for incredible damage to our families, our country, and our world? When will we realize we're so powerful that we can't "do our own thing" without affecting everything and everyone around us?

Men have got to realize that it isn't just the major abuses of power, like sinking a savings and loan or landing someone in the hospital, that leave lasting scars. All it takes is one razor-edged remark by a father, left unattended, perhaps simply unnoticed, and the biting pain can still sting after 40 years.

"Oh, come now," you may say. "One simple statement? Isn't that being too dramatic?"

We wish it were simply hyperbole. But listen to the reality in Larry's story, an echo of so many we've heard in our counseling office:

"When I was just five, my aunt came to visit us unexpectedly. This was my favorite aunt, particularly because the few times a year she came into town, she always brought me a present. And this visit was no exception.

"This time she gave me something I had longed for—a plastic ball and bat set. I rushed out to the garage where my father was, and where he spent most of his free time.

When will we realize we're so powerful that we can't 'do our own thing' without affecting everything and everyone around us?

"'Daddy, Daddy,' I cried, showing him my ball and bat. 'Would you come out and play ball with me?'

"He'd bent over the car, adjusting the carburetor for the hundredth time. When he heard my question, he straightened up and gave me a long, piercing look that I've never forgotten to this day.

"'Let's get something straight,' he said. '*I'm your father, not your friend.*'"

Something was lost that day that was never regained. Something was broken that was never repaired. Something was poisoned that was never purified.

Do you still think it's farfetched to say that a 5-year-old boy could remember a single incident into his forties? Listen to the testimony of a woman in her fifties, reflecting on a dad's broken promise when she was just 4 years old. The incident occurred more than 40 years ago, and yet look at the power her father's actions still carry.

"My parents divorced when I was four and my sister was seven. I remember crying at night, asking Mother why he had left and what we had done to make him go away.

"My father was gone for several months. But then, the night before Easter, we were told he was going to come and take us out to church and then spend the day with us.

"We both got up extra early that day and put on our newly purchased Easter dresses. We rushed through breakfast and then planted ourselves on top of the heating radiator that made a seat where we could look out our large picture window.

"There we sat, giggling and talking about how much fun we were going to have with our father. And there we sat all morning, through lunch, and on into the evening when we finally gave up.

"He never showed up, never even bothered to call. To this day, I can still remember the crushing hurt and disappointment I felt that Easter.

"I'm in my fifties now, and it has taken me years to come to understand that you really can depend on someone ... even God."

Men, it's time we faced up to being a large part of the problem with our families, our country, our world, and began joining together to become the leaders in solving what's wrong. Often, the problems we face come directly from our fathers or from some other important men in our lives. But regardless of the source, we ought to be on our knees in repentance, broken over what we've done and willing to face the fact that even if it's our brother who is the problem, it's our responsibility to help him.

Let's face it squarely: There's a dark side to our power as men.

But that's only one side. The potential for good is just as deep, just as lasting, and just as much within our reach. Positive memories can last just as long and remain just as vivid as negative ones.

MEMORIES THAT CAN BLOOM THROUGHOUT A LIFETIME

Sara, another friend of ours, tells a different story, a tale of a man who was too busy to learn to use his gold sword ... but took the time anyway. Someone like you. Someone like us. Not a large player in the fate of the world, but someone who knew that in his little corner of the universe, he could use his power to make a major difference.

After her father's death, Sara went through some of his personal things.

Opening his Bible, she came across a pressed rosebud and two ticket stubs. Suddenly, the memories came flooding back. During her insecure, unsettling, and terribly important teenage years, her father had picked up his gold sword and used his power for good.

"I grew up in a poor family in the late 1940s," Sara says. "My father loved us very much and worked extremely hard to keep five kids in shoes and clothes. But still, most of our clothes were hand-me-downs from the missionary barrel at church.

"During high school, I struck gold with a wealthy family at church who needed a baby-sitter. I saved my money, and then one night, I wrote up a special invitation to my father, asking if he would go out with me on a special 'date' the next night.

"My father responded by picking up flowers on his way home from work, then brushing off and putting on his only nice suit—usually reserved for weddings or funerals. 'After all,' he said, 'It's not often you get to go out with the

Great objects can be moved by small levers, and long years can be warmed or chilled by the lever of small happenings, small comments, and small encounters.

belle of the ball.'

"We went to a local restaurant and had hamburgers and chocolate milk-shakes. Then we went to see a show, and we walked home together, arm in arm.

"I'll never forget how he hugged me when we got home, and how he told me he loved me, prayed for me, and was proud of me."

Looking at those ticket stubs and the faded rose from a special night nearly half a century ago, Sara realized how the power of that memory had warmed her days and encouraged her heart through all the intervening years. No matter what others may have thought of her, her father thought she was "the belle of the ball." No matter what she accomplished or failed to accomplish, she could still close her eyes and see the pride glistening in her father's eyes.

The flowers may have faded, but the memories still bloom. As a five-year-old, she liked her father's attention. As a teenager, she longed for it. Now in her middle years, she still catches the fragrance of a loving father on the edge of a drifting memory and draws comfort from it.

It was just one evening. One incident. A few hours. A casual remark or two. Yet great objects can be moved by small levers. And long years can be warmed or chilled by the lever of small happenings, small comments, and small encounters.

That lever lies in a father's hand—in *your* hand. Whether we use it for good or bad or fail to use it at all does not change the fact that this awesome influence is in our grasp. No matter what we say or fail to say, we have that power. And we need to rally together to correct any damage and compound the good we can do in the lives of our wives and children.

No matter how you may feel today—as commanding as General Norman Schwarzkopf or as cowardly as the lion from Oz—in this book we want you to see that the gold sword you possess is the greatest power a man can have.

It's a power that can help you become the man you've always wanted to be.

A power your family longs for you to demonstrate.

A power that calls you to pick up two swords, but with one purpose: God's highest calling of love.

And our response?

"All right! I can see there's a gold sword I need to pick up and that I'm incredibly powerful in the life of my family! I do have great value when it comes to affecting generations for good. But now what do I do?"

One thing you *don't* have to do is go it alone. Let us give you some coaching so that you, with practice, can become a master of your gold sword; then get several "neighbors close at hand" to help you hold out your sword ... to become a promise keeper ... to use your power wisely as a godly man.

All that begins by actually creating your own gold sword. It's a unique process that draws on your wife and family members and leaves you with a tool you'll be proud to carry ... and they'll be glad you do.

CHAPTER 4

CREATING YOUR
OWN GOLD SWORD

Perhaps you feel defeated or discouraged after reading the preceding chapters. You may take inventory of your marriage and family and come out feeling you've dropped the ball. But whatever your situation, *it's not time to give up*. Beginning with this chapter, we want to show you how to come back, to stay on course, and to end up achieving a victory as good as your dreams.

History is full of apparent defeats that turned into tremendous victories. The early Christians overcame the lions. The United States fought back from the smoke and ashes of Pearl Harbor to win a World War. America also lost the race with the Soviets to put the first man in space, but then the nation rallied to put a man on the moon. You even see it in the Atlanta Braves and Minnesota Twins baseball teams. Both were in absolute last place one year and then tops in their respective leagues the next, battling it out in the World Series of 1991.

Great turnarounds don't just happen. They come as the direct result of learning from fiery trials and, out of the ashes, forging a plan of action that works. Our friend Dave Dravecky, in his wonderful book *Comeback*, tells how he overcame great odds and still held on to his gold sword. And while it's not on your bookshelf yet, someday you'll read one of the greatest comeback stories I (Gary) know of—the story of what happened with my good friend Rich D'Ortinzio.

The way Rich crawled out of one of life's deepest pits, a pit he'd dug for himself, illustrates the secret found in every great turnaround. What's more, his family illustrates the overall goal of this book as they reached level ground, joined with a few good friends to keep from falling back into the pit, and then moved up to a life of recovery, restoration, and fulfillment.

Rich's story begins in the summer of 1969. After a conflict-free courtship and wedding, he and Penny were driving back to their newly rented love nest, a small apartment on the outskirts of Detroit. For Penny, this was her dream come true. She had a husband who loved her, a place to call her own, and an escape from the craziness and abuse of 18 years in a terribly dysfunctional family.

That's what makes a functional family— not the absence of mistakes, but the willingness to talk about the mistakes that were made and then form a clear plan for a fulfilling future.

Penny came from a home where the silver sword ruled. Her opinions were dismissed, her rights violated. Her deep longing for acceptance was thrown back in her face. She endured nearly two decades of loneliness and emotional struggles.

Penny remembered being six years old (a time when most children laugh away the days and are tucked into bed with sweet dreams) and lying awake at night, wishing she'd die so she didn't have to face the pain anymore.

But all that unhappiness had finally been set aside. At last she had found a sensitive man, one who listened to and accepted her; one who cared for what she thought and felt; a man who valued who she was inside, not just her looks, and encouraged her to become more than she had dreamed possible—that is, until they crossed over Ambassador Bridge into Detroit coming back from their honeymoon.

"I don't know exactly what happened," Rich told me, "but I remember distinctly that something clicked off in my mind when we crossed that bridge."

What clicked off? Only the sensitivity ... the willingness to hear her side of things ... the unconditional acceptance ... the emotional control that had held back his raging anger.

"I never knew he had a temper until we got back from our honeymoon," Penny said. "That's when he got so mad at me, he punched his *first* hole in the wall."

From 1969 until 1981, Penny found she had traded one place of abuse for another. She also brought two sons into the world, and they faced verbal attacks as well.

Rich was a union man, a fiery Italian. His days were spent working at the railway yard, his nights at home terrorizing the family. He became a master at using the silver sword to browbeat and crush his family.

"You're a fat mess!" he'd yell at his older son, who at seven years of age was ten years away from exchanging rolls of baby fat for solid muscle and all-state honors in football and baseball. "It's your fault I'm so unhappy," he'd rage at his captive, frightened audience. "You're the reason my life is being ruined."

But even a hurricane eventually loses its brute force and its power to keep people in hiding.

Penny had always searched for a way of escape. Since childhood, suicide had been one option. But deep in her heart, she knew there must be some way . . . *some-one* who could offer a way of release.

A woman is drawn to a man who provides loving leadership but resists one who makes self-centered demands.

For a time during their courtship, she had convinced herself that it was Rich. But in her heart of hearts, she knew God was the one who really loved her, who would never betray her, who could be that best friend she longed for. And at a Bible study she had been invited to by some neighborhood friends, she learned she could know Him in a personal way. Shocked at the simplicity of the gospel, she accepted Christ as her Lord and Savior. Then things got worse.

"I would call her a Jesus freak," Rich said. "I'd ridicule her for taking the children to church and slam her every way I could about being religious." Tears gathered in the corners of his eyes, and he paused for a few seconds to regain his composure. Then he shook his head and added, "I can't believe I treated her that way."

But he did—until the elevator finally stopped going down in his life one spring day in 1981. Confronted by the reality of change in Penny's life, and totally bankrupt in his own, he finally faced who he was ... who he'd become. It was a terrible picture. But leave it to the Master to pick up the paintbrush and rework a picture of anger and hostility into one of hope, high potential, and promise.

Rich, too, trusted Christ as Savior. But if it was an elevator ride down to the emotional depths, it has been one step at a time to get to higher ground. "I really didn't begin to change for several months," Rich said. "I knew I needed to be different. But I didn't really want to face all the changes I needed to make, and I didn't know how.

"Before I became a Christian, I can't ever remember reading a book outside of school. But after I met Christ, I started reading Christian books all the time to figure out what to do right for a change. Then one day, Penny handed me a book she wanted me to read. It wasn't a Christian book, but one she said I needed to read anyway. Its title? *Men Who Hate Women, and the Women Who Love Them.*

"For a long time, I refused to even pick it up. To be honest, I was scared by the title. But finally, after her leaving it around for months, I was at home all alone one day, bored, waiting for work. That's when I said to myself, 'Oh, all right,' picked it up, and never made it past chapter 3.

"In fact, I still haven't finished the book after all these years. That's because I saw myself so clearly in those first three chapters.

"I was destroying my wife and sons with my anger and abuse, and I fell on my knees and thanked God for humbling me. From that point on, I was ready to do whatever it took to learn whatever I needed to know and be the husband and father He wanted me to be."

SWORD SCHOOL BEGINS

It was some years ago now that Rich fell to his knees, and nearly that long since I (Gary) have had the privilege of calling him one of my closest friends. At the time, our sons were playing for the same high school football team, and Rich came into my life when he was broken, sorrowful—and teachable. It's a tough place to end up ... but a great place to begin.

Rich asked for help in becoming the man he knew he should be and wasn't being consistently, even though he was now a Christian. And it's been one of Norma's and my greatest joys to disciple and encourage Rich and Penny ever since.

My time with Rich has taken the form of weekly lessons in using the gold sword with his family. We hold each other accountable for how we're doing at meeting seven different goals in using that sword, each goal a focus of discussion in the next two chapters.

But before Rich was ready to rush over, pick up the sword, and start swinging it around (or before you jump ahead to the next chapter!), he had to put something crucial into practice.

Before he launched into what became years of everyday effort to strengthen his family life, Rich and Penny had to do the same thing that turned America around in World War II and then caused it to run away with the space race—the same thing that can take a team from last place to a world championship.

Namely, out of the ashes of defeat, they needed to set a *clear direction* that would inspire, direct, and push them toward a deeper, more meaningful way of relating as a couple. And closely linked with developing this personalized plan was the need for the strong support of others who could help them accomplish their aim.

Without that crucial first step, Rich and Penny would end up fighting each other instead of agreeing on the lifetime direction they should travel together.

MEN WITH A CLEAR GOAL

Ask any of the people who fought in World War II or in Desert Storm, and they'll tell you they had an overall plan that was clearly set before them and an unmistakable spirit of teamwork in accomplishing their goals. In one case, the goal was finishing a fight with Hitler and Hirohito that had been brought to our soil, and in the other it was joining with the world to drive a madman out of tiny Kuwait.

Those men and women, with their clear goals and close-knit teams, won in a mighty way. And while no less valiant, those who fought in Vietnam were *not* given a clear, overall goal that could lift their spirits when times were tough or rally a nation behind them.

For Rich and Penny, the turnaround began by taking a careful inventory of where their life had been. They also looked closely at where their life was at present and how the past had affected their children.

As a result, they realized that Mario, their older son, had been deeply affected by his father's silver sword. He struggled with sharing his feelings and could be rough and demanding, just as his father was for so many years. But now he and the whole family have a goal of working to overcome that attitude, and he's learning along with his father how to pick up the gold sword. That decision can keep the chains of a negative past from being passed down as a part of Mario's future.

Michael, their younger son, saw the tremendous changes in his parents, and as a result, he's planning to become a counselor some day. He wants to help other people deal with the negative effects of the silver sword and gain a clear plan for using the gold one.

That's what makes a functional family—not the absence of mistakes, but the willingness, the openness and honesty, to talk about the mistakes that were made and then form a clear plan for building a positive, fulfilling future.

That's our goal for every man and woman reading this book. We all need to take careful inventory of where we are, of what negative effects we may have had on our spouses, children, and friends. And then we need to look carefully at the future we really want to have, set goals, and practice a plan that can move us from frustration to fulfillment.

TWO FOUR-LETTER WORDS THAT SPELL LOVE

If our family goals are going to help us find the fulfillment we all want, however, they have to be based on the foundation of God's plan for the husband-wife relationship. One key biblical passage describing that plan—and two words in particular—have been the subject of much misunderstanding and controversy in recent years. Let us explain what we've come to understand about these extremely important words and try to clear up some of that confusion so we can set goals consistent with His will in this vital area.

The passage we refer to is Ephesians 5, where the ideas of *headship* and *submission* are used to define the roles of husband and wife, respectively. Mention either of those terms in many conversations today and it's as if you've uttered a four-letter word. Talk of a man's being a godly leader and his wife a willing completer and supporter can turn some women's eyes red. But those concepts are two of the most powerful and honoring in all the Scriptures. They also establish the foundation needed for setting and meeting mutually-agreed-upon goals.

We want God's plan to be the one that guides our homes. We also understand that when we know the truth, it will set us free, not push any man or woman into unhealthy bondage. When God speaks of headship and submission, in no way is He endorsing "lording it over" others. That's the world's way of handling headship. But as you'll see, the Scriptures set forth a new, distinctively different pattern for building a successful marriage.

With that in mind, let's try to gain a clear understanding of this passage to see how it can enrich our relationships and inspire us to be the men and women God called us to be, people who hold high a gold sword.

MEN CALLED TO BIBLICAL HEADSHIP

To the world, headship in the home has come to mean the dictatorial, demeaning authority of an unchanged J.D. or Rich D'Ortinzio. But from God's Word, it's clear that a man is to lead in one thing: love.

"Husbands, love your wives, just as Christ loved the church and gave himself up for her to make her holy, cleansing her by the washing with water through the word."[1] Again we read, "In this same way, husbands ought to love their wives as their own bodies."[2]

Our marching orders as men, direct from our Commander-in-Chief, call for us to take the high ground of love, to fight our way up a hill just as Christ did when He laid down His life for us.

J.D. and Rich didn't have any problem with expecting—actually demanding—that their wives submit to their leadership. The only problem was, their leadership wasn't anywhere near biblical headship! To them, the instruction for women to "submit to your husbands"[3] meant "Make my dinner, go get the paper, and keep the kids from bothering me while I'm watching TV." Their goal was self-centered satisfaction, not the type of love where each person is laying down his life for the other!

A woman is drawn to a man who provides loving leadership but resists one who makes self-centered demands. We have yet to meet a woman who isn't willing to follow her husband's leadership when he's committed to doing what's best for her and their family.

Still not convinced? A little confused? Please, keep going, and see just how a man's leadership, linked with a woman's support, begins to make perfect sense.

WIVES CALLED TO SUBMIT TO THEIR HUSBANDS' LOVING LEADERSHIP

Submission has come to stand for knuckling under, swallowing your real feelings, backing yourself into a corner, turning off your brain, and being dysfunctional and codependent. But that's exactly the *opposite* of what the Bible means when it tells wives to submit to their husbands.

In Ephesians 5, before wives are called to submit, we read, "Submit to one another out of reverence for Christ."[4] In Greek, the original language of the New Testament, being "subject to" another person was actually a military term. It's a word that speaks of support, voluntary allegiance, and cooperation. It leaves room for creativity and even questioning while maintaining a high commitment. It carries with it none of the damaging misconceptions of high control or manipulation but instead connotes teamwork and mutual respect.

For a wife, submission involves responding to her husband's leadership "as to the Lord"[5]—*not as an inferior, but as one committed to a mutual goal that is worthy of her life*.

The idea is like President Bush calling on Congress to authorize military action against Saddam Hussein to drive him out of Kuwait. Then General Powell, the chairman of the Joint Chiefs of Staff, responds with an "Aye, Aye, Sir" and contacts an overall commander, General Schwarzkopf, to pull together a plan.

Next, General Schwarzkopf calls together his commanders, and they in turn issue orders through every layer of the military centered on a clear purpose: "We're going to drive that man and his army out of Kuwait!" Each group in turn says "Aye, aye," adds its own creativity and effort to the overall plan, and works its hardest to fulfill the primary goal laid down by the leaders.

You didn't sense feelings of inferiority when pictures came in of General Schwarzkopf walking among his troops, shaking their hands, and praying with them before they went into battle. You sensed only loyalty, clarity of purpose, and a mutual willingness to serve. And you sensed something else between him and his men—a genuine love. But someone still had to take the lead. They knew it. They needed it. And it brought them the quickest and most decisive victory in American military history.

Loving headship and voluntary submission. The message of Ephesians 5 is that husbands and wives need to get their plans clearly established. What hill are you going to take as a family? What plateau do you want to reach with your children? Where are you headed as a couple in the next year? the next five years? over your lifetime?

DETERMINING YOUR DIRECTION AS A COUPLE

Without first determining your direction as a couple and as parents, you'll never reach the level of fulfillment you could. In fact, the absence of clear goals is one of the biggest problems we see in families around the world. Husbands and wives simply do not know where they're going, and without clear, overall goals of headship and submission, guiding a relationship can be impossible.

One of the first things we did with Rich and Penny was to help them agree on some goals—goals they could both commit themselves to wholeheartedly; goals that made the biblical concepts of headship and submission not only understandable, but also necessary to their success.

As we'd done with our own families years ago, we had them write out their goals in the form of a family constitution. Why? Look at the scramble to form new democratic governments in the republics of the former Soviet Union. What's the first thing they draft as they're changing their government from one of oppression to newfound freedom? A clear, written constitution that will guide them in the years to come as our constitution has done for us.

The same principle is important for governing a family. When Norma and I (Gary) first came up with our own family constitution, we had six agreed-upon goals. I was to take the leadership in establishing them in our home, and Norma wanted to help complete and support me in that role.

That early process of writing our constitution was crucial for a number of reasons. It helped us both agree on what was best for us as a couple, and for our actions as parents. It also solidified what we believed God would have us do with our relationship.

Our efforts in putting that plan down and then practicing it faithfully have paid off in dividends of family closeness and unity that I would have never thought possible. And it came through the two of us setting a mutual direction, me taking the lead in accomplishing that goal, and Norma submitting to that plan and supporting me. Only recently, when I met with a biblical scholar (our pastor, Darryl DelHousaye) and worked through an even clearer understanding of Ephesians 5, did I see why what we did was so powerful.[6]

After talking for several hours with our resident New Testament expert, I headed home for the day. Norma was in the bedroom when I got there, and before I could tell her what we'd been talking about, she said something that shocked me: "Gary, do you know what I really love doing? It's helping you reach your goals. When they get foggy for you, it affects me somehow."

Goose bumps formed on my arms as I heard her describe her desire for us to have clear goals, for me to take the lead in accomplishing them, and for her to support me in every way. The wise wife in the Song of Solomon had said the same thing to her husband centuries ago: "Draw me after you and let us run together!"[7]

45

Since that time, I've asked several thousand women at our seminars if they enjoy helping their husbands reach goals that benefit their families. And I still haven't found a negative response!

AN EXAMPLE OF GOAL-SETTING LIVED OUT

Norma and I know now that our fifth goal did more to build strength, unity, and love in our family than anything else. For without realizing it, by practicing it we were laying the foundation for the highest thing God calls us to do. What was that goal? "To honor God, others, and His creation." Yet *honor* sounds like a simple concept. Why is it so powerful?

It is God's ultimate will for us to love Him and to love others.[8] And love grows out of an attitude of honoring someone. When we decide someone is valuable, that decision alone is a major first step in acting out our love for the person.

Scripture puts it this way in speaking of our spiritual affections: "For where your treasure is, there your heart will be also."[9] In other words, those things that we highly value are the very things that will capture our hearts.

To honor others is to "place high value" on them. Another form of the idea is to be "weighty" or "heavy." So honoring those in our homes means making a decision that they're heavyweights, worthy of great importance and appreciation. On the other hand, to dishonor people actually means treating their thoughts or feelings as if they carry only as much weight as mist or steam.

A husband who wants to love his wife as Christ loved the church makes the decision that she is worthy of honor, high respect, and a top position in his heart and life.[10] The same goes for any father, mother, child, or friend.

When Norma and I set honor as one of our everyday family goals, it revolutionized our relationships with God and each other. Each night at the dinner table, when the kids were younger, we'd take time to go through our family constitution and ask how well we'd done at honoring God and each other.

With the goal of honor always in front of us, combined with the loving accountability at mealtimes, we avoided falling into dishonoring patterns that can ruin a family's closeness. (In the next two chapters, we'll see that this is one of seven elements that should be part of each family's gold sword.)

The decision to honor others had a powerful impact on our children as well. Calling a brother or sister a name was now seen as dishonoring. And because they knew our family goals (we had clearly communicated them, even placing them in written form on the kitchen wall), they began to see their actions as either helping to meet or keeping them from meeting those goals.

Helping a brother pick up his toys was honoring, and they began to see how that moved us closer toward our goal. So did not taking the Lord's name in vain; attending church as a priority; not hurtfully teasing friends; finishing homework. As everyday actions were viewed in terms of whether we hit the target of honor, our focus was kept on what was best and most loving in our home.

While we weren't aware of it at the time, we were actually fulfilling a basic biblical commandment: "Whatever is true, whatever is *honorable*, whatever is right, whatever is pure, whatever is lovely, whatever is of good repute, if there is any excellence and if anything worthy of praise, let your mind *dwell* on these things."[11]

Our goal of honor extended beyond our home as well. For example, we taught our children that honor should even be given to things outside our home ... like hotel beds.

One of the Smalley family's favorite things to do is travel. When the kids were younger, we'd load everyone in our mini-mobile home and head off for a weekend speaking engagement. I'd speak on Friday night and Saturday until noon, and then I'd join the rest of the family at the hotel we'd picked out for a mini-vacation.

Almost without fail, one of the first things our kids would want to do when they hit the room was to bounce on the beds. And if it was humanly possible, they'd bounce from one bed to the other.

However, as we began to take honor seriously as a family goal, the idea of bouncing on someone else's bed, even if it was the hotel's, seemed dishonoring. So when we hit the hotel and they began to bounce, I'd say, "Shouldn't we ask someone like the hotel manager if we can play trampoline with the beds?"

They would always complain, but they'd drag themselves down the hall and talk to the hotel manager, and he always gave them permission. They'd come back whooping and hollering, "He said yes!" And in an instant, they would be bouncing off the beds and the walls (with Mom and Dad as spotters, of course).

We wanted to teach them how important it is to honor other people's possessions. And it's a lesson each of the children took to heart.

By making honor one of our agreed-upon goals, we were actually forcing ourselves to focus on the positive, on what builds relationships, not on what breaks them down. And something equally powerful took place as well. By submitting to the goal of honor and helping each other reach it, *we became a unified team in our marriage and with our children.* Headship and submission. Working in harmony, I was taking up the gold sword, and as a family we were taking our own "hill of honor."

A TREMENDOUS BY-PRODUCT OF SETTING CLEAR GOALS: UNITY

When goals are clear in a marriage, couples gain a sense of unity that isn't possible any other way. Agreeing on the goal of honor gave me something to strive toward, to set the pace for, in our family. It provided a natural, healthy way in which to take the biblical lead in our home. For Norma, it became equally natural to submit to my leadership in honoring her and the children, not surprisingly because it was her goal as well!

With the goal of honoring the children in place, there was no hesitancy in her saying "Aye, Aye!" and both of us going to bat for what was best for our family. Now she could come alongside and support me, using her natural strengths and gifts as a woman. And I could accept her support without feeling threatened or insecure.

For example, our daughter, Kari, might come home from school one day feeling dejected, and I might fail to notice her mood. But because our goal was

Taking the time to set clear goals as a couple is one of the most powerful, unifying, and loving things you can do.

to have a home with honor, where everyone felt valuable, Norma could point out Kari's mood to me with her superior sensitivity, and I could then go in and encourage and support our daughter using my strengths.

Mutual submission to God made us a team. Working hard to accomplish a goal of honor jointly, we found a deepening closeness that was a direct result of first setting a clear goal together.

That's why, when I first sat down with Rich, I told him about the crucial need to get a clear, mutually-agreed-upon battle plan with clear goals so that all his and Penny's efforts would be as a team from that point on. *In short, taking the time to set clear goals as a couple is one of the most powerful, unifying, and loving things you can do.*

Once those goals are set, a second key helps us to stay on track: We need to allow each person in the home, spouse or child, to ask openly, "How are we doing at meeting our agreed-upon goals?"

Such honest, loving inspection is vital not only between family members, but also between close friends who are helping each other accomplish their own individual family goals.

On one trip I took with Rich and Penny to the beautiful art community of Sedona, Arizona, Penny began describing how difficult it was for her deal with her relatives. Each time she had to attend a family function, it brought back all those memories of a tragic, abusive background, and her perspective and attitude would turn sour for days.

Love grows out of an attitude of honoring someone.

In the middle of her sharing some deep feelings, Rich shot out, "Penny, when are you going to grow up? Come on! You're *letting* your relatives affect you that way. Either don't get together with your family, or just don't let it bother you!"

Rich meant well. As a man, he'd seen a problem (Family functions bring back bad memories), come up with a quick solution (Don't visit your family if it bothers you, or just don't let it bother you), and even provided extra motivation (Come on! Grow up!). But Penny didn't need him to put on his coach's hat and whistle; she needed his understanding and comfort.

I'm sure he thought he had done the right thing, but by the silence Penny retreated into for the rest of the trip, it was obvious he hadn't. Without realizing it, he had labeled her as a child, rebuked her for having normal feelings, and then given her an impossible task. If she could have turned off her emotional spigot at a family gathering, she would have done so long ago! Instead of helping her gain the acceptance she needed to finally move past the sting of a difficult situation, Rich had increased her feelings of isolation.

I knew that honor was one of the goals Rich had set for his family. I also knew he had just done a very dishonoring thing in blasting his wife, even if he meant it for good. And that left me only one thing to do as a committed, supportive friend (the same thing John and I regularly ask each other to do).

When we got back to Phoenix, the next chance I had, I told him point blank, "Rich, you did something on our trip that really seemed to dishonor Penny. Instead of encouraging her to share her feelings and then floating down the river with her in her emotional boat, you ran her boat right up on the rocks! When she sees her mother and it discourages her, you should take that opportunity to encourage her, not blast her. If you're going to present Penny one day as whole and complete,[12] you've got to learn to provide her the support she needs to deal with family trials."

Strong words. But they were met with an openness that is something I love and appreciate about Rich. He quickly saw what he'd done, admitted he'd blown it (to me and, that night, to Penny), and got right back in line the next day with the goal of honor before him.

Healthy families are those that can ask the question, "Are we meeting our goals?" Dysfunctional families commonly answer with an emphatic "No!" but feel powerless to say or do anything about it. They don't know where they're headed, and there is misunderstanding or even a raging battle about headship and support. But perhaps the greatest negative factor in a hurting family is this spoken or unspoken rule: "Let's not talk about our problems. Let's keep our pain a secret."

Trying to cover up dishonoring actions with a family secret can destroy a family. That's why I've given Norma, Rich, John, my own children, and several other friends permission to be open with me if I ever dishonor them or they see me dishonoring my family in any way. They know my goals, the highest one being honor. And I'm encouraged by their pointing out areas where I need to grow.

As men, we've seen how powerful we are in the lives of our loved ones and the kind of damage we can do. We've also seen how the gold sword of personal power can help undo a multitude of wrongs. But it won't happen if we don't first have clear goals for our families.

In the next two chapters, we'll describe seven goals that we believe make up the gold sword. As you read, you'll get a clear picture of this sword that every man should pick up and use daily.

CHAPTER 5

SEVEN REFLECTIONS
OF THE GOLD SWORD

PART 1

W e're thrilled you've read this far, and we're doubly excited if you're planning to re-examine your life's goals with your mate, perhaps even writing them out together for the first time.

In this chapter and the next, we want to give you a list of seven basics that make up *our* gold sword. These fundamentals, captured in written form, can become a family constitution. And while you may adopt all seven of the basics we've listed, the real power comes in writing your own agreed-upon marriage and family plan. You may decide to toss out some of our concepts and add others that fit your particular situation.

We've already seen that *headship* and *submission* are military terms. Taking the time now to forge your own gold sword (as you write out your own family constitution) will be a little like "basic training." Once you've finished this project, however, you'll have a personal plan to show you how to lead and what to support together as husband and wife. Winning the battle begins with basic training.

BASIC TRAINING IN USING THE GOLD SWORD

Boot camp is misery with a purpose in mind. Eight weeks of grueling physical and psychological stress are designed to turn a group of individuals into something more than the sum of its parts—a team, a unit whose members have learned to depend on each other, support each other, and even lay down their lives for each other if necessary.

In large part, that's the same goal we're calling men to across the country. Not eight weeks of running with a rifle through the mud or having a drill instructor motivate you by standing one inch from your face, but joining with a group of men and committing to stand together, train together, and go to the wall together, if necessary, to do what's right before God and our families.[1]

In the Marines, attending basic training is just a starting point, and it means going to places like Quantico, Camp Pendleton, or Parris Island. For many of us, reading this book, doing the exercises, and working to apply the principles each day can be basic training. We'll be laying down new skills and beefing up habits that can make a lasting difference in our relationships.

Others, however, may need the extra boost of a concentrated time of training. That might involve attending our "Love Is a Decision" seminar or one of the many other fine seminars like Campus Crusade's "Family Life" conference. Many churches hold weekend retreats on family-life skills led by outstanding speakers like Tim Kimmel, Steve Farrar, Jay Carty, Bill Butterworth, Dave Simmons, John Nieder, Randy Carlson, Kevin Leman, Larry Crabb, Neil Anderson, Gary Oliver, and others.

There's nothing magical about a weekend or longer of intensive training, but there is something motivational about it. That's especially true if you go with a group of men and their wives who can become a mutual support group to help each other stay strong in the battle. (We'll talk more about the importance of this in chap. 12.)

If traveling to one of these seminars is out of the question, try to obtain their materials in audio or video form. Then gather your own group and hold a mini-seminar in your home. (Actually, that's what our "Homes of Honor" small-group study material, which we'll discuss later, was designed for.)

What will you learn by going through a time of concentrated study in the basics? At our seminar, we present key principles of handling the gold sword—many of the same principles we cover in the following pages. These principles come out of more than 20 years of study, counseling, and interviewing couples and families. This past year alone, we surveyed more than 14,000 people nationwide who attended our seminars, asking them what makes strong, lasting relationships. Their responses, poured through the grid of the Scriptures, give us the 7 principles we feel are basic to carrying the gold sword. But they're only the basics.

In the Army, once you complete basic training, you're sent to AIT,

Advanced Individual Training, to specialize in some skill that will make you even more valuable to the team. For some it might be clerk's school, for others telecommunications. Another man might go to light artillery school or air defense artillery school.

Every man needs to go on to "AIT" in handling the gold sword as well, working on whatever principles require the most work in his own life or in another area of training that doesn't fit within our list. Some men will need to attend Advanced Communications School, learning practical methods of opening up and sharing on a level deeper than the weather report. Others will need Advanced Finance School to master the disciplines of writing and sticking to a budget and planning for the future in a wise, biblical way. Still others may need to go to Advanced Forgiveness School and deal with hurts from their fathers that are making it difficult to be godly men.

We'll talk about how you can design your own advanced training program, as well as a way to continually sharpen your sword. But it's up to each of us to get a plan that fits our individual situations and needs.

Ready to buckle your chin strap and get into the battle? It begins with the basics in handling the gold sword. Each principle will be like turning the sword slightly and gaining a different reflection of light off the blade. And at the end of each of the seven sections, we'll offer some suggestions for what you can do in the way of AIT in that area.

Let's begin by taking a firm grip on the handle. It's pictured in a crucial concept called *honor*. We touched on this idea in chapter 4, but we want to take you deeper into its meaning and value. We highly recommend that this concept become a part of your family constitution in some form.

1. Deciding to Honor Our Loved Ones

The most important ingredient in a successful family is honoring one another. Grabbing hold of honor is like getting a solid grip on your gold sword. We've written an entire book about this concept,[2] but for the purpose of this book, we'll break it down into four specific tasks.

First, honoring others begins with giving honor to God. As we mentioned earlier, *honor* means attaching high value, and in this case highest value, to someone. We've devoted an entire chapter (chap. 14) to God's role in our handling of the gold sword. But to help you understand how we go about honoring Him, consider a familiar activity that takes place each year.

For most men, watching or listening to the Super Bowl isn't optional—it's a requirement! Pictures came back from Desert Shield of men huddled in camou-flaged tents—in the midst of war preparations—cheering on the Bills and the Giants on televisions powered by portable generators. Why? Because to the average man, the Super Bowl is something of high value! And the men who play in it are granted a place of high esteem.

That's the same principle of honor we need to apply to God and His Word, but giving Him much higher importance. Whatever we value, whatever we count as a treasure, whatever we make a "Super Bowl" in our minds, that's where our feelings will be. We won't forget to pray if sharing our feelings and burdens with God becomes of highest value to us. Reading the Bible ceases to be drudgery when we place "*Super*-Super Bowl" status on His inspired Word.

The psalmist wrote, "Thy word I have *treasured* in my heart, that I may not

Whatever we value, whatever we count as a treasure, whatever we make a "Super Bowl" in our minds, that's where our feelings will be.

sin against Thee"[3] and "I have rejoiced in the way of Thy testimonies, as much as in *all* riches."[4] In other words, if we have difficulty in honoring God, one main reason is that He and His Word aren't as valuable to us as other things.

It's great to love sports. During the Super Bowl, we'll be right there with you, Doritos and Diet Coke in hand, cheering away. But let's never forget that we're called to "set our affections" on Him and give Him the highest honor of all.

What's more, our wives love knowing that pleasing God is a priority for us. That alone can strengthen our relationship and add greatly to the next aspect of honor.

Second, honor involves making the commitment to build security into our loved ones' lives. We strengthen our grip on the gold sword when our families consis-tently feel secure in our love. This means saying to them that next to God, no one and nothing is more important than them. They have our commitment for life. And then we have to back up those statements with a supportive attitude that takes our words to their emotional bank and earns interest.

After speaking with thousands of women over the years, we're still amazed at how consistently the concept of security comes up on their lists of "most desirable traits" in a husband. Your wife needs to know that nothing on earth will separate you from her. That you took your marriage vows seriously on your wedding day. That you're committed to formulating a clear plan for growth for the entire family and then taking the lead in accomplishing it, no matter what the cost!

This desire for security isn't unique to American culture. As I (Gary) have ministered from Rumania to Africa, I've heard women express this same deep-seated need.

At one conference in Ghana, Africa, I saw men become so convicted about the need to provide security and honor to their wives that they'd stand up in the meeting and say, "My wife is a queen, and from now on, I'm going to treat her like that." Joyful smiles broke out on wives' faces throughout the packed auditorium!

But honor isn't just a matter of expressing it to our wives in public. It's perhaps even more powerful when it comes in private.

Recently, we've been honored to have as a co-sponsor of our seminars the wonderful people at DaySpring Greeting Cards. Why link up with them? Because women tell us that receiving a special card from their husbands is one of the primary ways they feel most honored.

Children get a sense of security and love from such cards, too—in honor of a good grade, a sports achievement, a nice art project, any all-out effort regardless of the outcome, or for no particular reason at all. Words of love and encouragement are always appreciated, and especially so when we've gone to the time and trouble to say them in writing.

Recently, at a gathering of almost 400 men, all leaders in their churches across the country, I was struck by a thought about honor that came to me right when I was speaking. I was saying that most men get really excited about symbols of accomplishment: golf trophies, tennis medals, diplomas, or mounted fish or game.

Spontaneously, I mentioned that I had recently caught a 27-inch Dolly Varden trout on a trip to Alaska and had just mounted it on my wall. And then I said, to their laughter, "I don't have a big picture of Norma at either my home or work office. But I've got trout I've caught mounted in both places!"

As the laughter poured in, my words suddenly caught in my throat. I had to stop and admit how amazing it was that I had never thought about that contrast before. Norma is of much higher value to me than any of the things I might accomplish, catch, or mount. Yet those "things" were more prominently displayed on my walls.

Rest assured that by the time you read this book, two beautifully framed pictures of Norma will be hanging in prominent places both at home and at work.

Third, honoring others involves verbally praising them. We need this as much as our loved ones. Several years ago, I (Gary) was walking by Norma's office at our ministry when I overheard a conversation she was having with a senior pastor of a large church. She wasn't trying to sell him on my speaking abilities or how humorous or inspiring our seminar might be. She was simply praising me for being a good father and husband, someone who tried hard to put into practice what he taught.

It was an unsolicited compliment, an accidentally overheard bit of praise from my wife. Yet after several years, I still remember it clearly! And I can recall many other acts of encouragement from Norma as well.

Just today, she called and told me she loved me and was praying for me as I

By God's design, honor involves praising each other regularly.

was away working on this book. She even told me she was going to stop what she was doing and write down several stories I might be able to use. I can't tell you how encouraged and uplifted I felt knowing she was with me in this project, supporting me fully!

By God's design, honor involves praising each other regularly. In the 8 short chapters of the Song of Solomon, God's blueprint for a strong relationship in the Old Testament, Solomon praised his bride more than 30 times, and she praised him a nearly equal amount!

Fourth, we honor others by protecting them. Norma is not the most aggressive person in the world, and there have been times when she tried to return an item to some store, only to have the clerk intimidate her. Knowing her resulting dread of returning items, I (Gary) have taken it upon myself to return some things for her if she requests it.

It seems like such a small thing, but every time I do it, Norma has thanked me for doing it and, indirectly, for my protection of her. Some men need to give their wives healthy protection from relatives or in-laws who are far too dominating; from a critical neighbor; or from some other source of irritation. The idea is not to fight every battle for them or take away their confidence that they can face tough issues on their own. Rather, it's another way to support them that says, "I'm with you, and I'll go to bat for you if you need me to."

Put God first. Then security, praise, and protection. These four aspects of honor make up the handle of our gold sword. And the tighter we grasp it, the more skillfully we'll be able to wield the sword.

After reading this first section and evaluating where you're at, you may decide you need to enroll in AIT in honoring others. If so, our ideas on going deeper in this area come next. But remember, it's *your* plan that counts. So take the time to evaluate our suggestions and even seek the counsel of others, formulating a tailor-made plan you can make part of your family constitution.

ADVANCED INDIVIDUAL TRAINING IN HONOR

Summary statement of this section:

Honor is placing high value on God or another person. It's the decision we make that someone has great worth and is a priceless treasure. Out of that decision and God's power comes our ability to genuinely and consistently love others.

Self-evaluation:

Rate yourself on these crucial elements of honoring God, your mate, or your children:

	Needs work				Doing Great		
Placing God first	1	2	3	4	5	6	7
Providing security	1	2	3	4	5	6	7
Giving regular praise	1	2	3	4	5	6	7
Providing protection	1	2	3	4	5	6	7

This simple evaluation can be the basis for discussion between you and your spouse, a vital way to sharpen your sword. But an honest personal assessment is the important first step.

Write down a personal affirmation statement of your intent to honor:

What's an affirmation statement? It's a statement of purpose and intent that captures your goals for your actions and words. It's a statement of your hopes and desires, even if you're still growing toward them.

In some ways, an affirmation statement is a statement of faith: "the assurance of things hoped for, the conviction of things not seen."[5]

Remember, you can tailor affirmation statements to fit your own words and goals. Just be sure to make them positive, oriented to the present, and encouraging. (If you write them in the future tense, change can be left to the future as well.) And then, like seeds of faith planted in your heart, positive actions will follow your biblical goals.

Sample Affirmation Statement:

(Affirming our desire to give God highest honor in our lives)
   God is at the top of everything in my life.
Your affirmation: _____

_____

_____

_____

(Affirming our need to provide security to our spouses)
   Next to God, my mate is the most important person on this earth to me, higher than anyone or anything else.
Your affirmation: _____

_____

_____

_____

(Affirming our commitment to praise our loved ones)
   It's natural for me to verbalize my love and appreciation for others.
Your affirmation: _____

_____

_____

_____

(Affirming our need to provide healthy protection)
   I regularly stand up and protect my family when they need me.
Your affirmation: _____

_____

_____

_____

Once your affirmation statements on this and the other parts of the gold sword are complete, you can write them all down on a three-by-five card and carry them with you—something we do everywhere we go. We appreciate the constant reminder of who we're claiming to be by faith, and our lists give us a direction, a positive purpose, and built-in accountability, all at the same time.

Write out your own marriage plan regarding honor:

If you agree that honor will be a significant part of your plan (family constitution), take the time here to write out your goal to honor as if it were an actual contract. Then read it out loud, and revise it as you and your wife agree. Continue to revise, expand, and amplify it throughout your life together. Include your children whenever possible.

_____

_____

_____

_____

_____

_____

_____

RESOURCES FOR HONORING OTHERS

Here's a listing of various books and tapes of ours and others that we recommend to help you grow in this area. You'll find a similar list for each of the seven aspects of the gold sword.

Books

Dennis and Barbara Rainey, *Building Your Mate's Self-Esteem* (San Bernardino, Cal.: Here's Life, 1986).

Gary Smalley and John Trent, *The Blessing* and *The Gift of Honor* (Nashville: Nelson, 1986, 1987).

Audio and video tapes

"Homes of Honor" small-group series. This is a resource we've just completed that takes the basic principles of our "Love Is a Decision" seminar and puts them in small-group form. Many groups and pastors around the country have helped us test and refine this material. Session 3 explores the principle of honor. (Information on the program is available through the Today's Family office by writing to P.O. Box 22111, Phoenix, AZ 85028, or calling 602-443-8682.)

After you finish reading about all seven aspects of the gold sword, *if this is the first AIT you want to take, pick one book and one tape you want to use in this area.* Then ask a friend to hold you accountable by asking you one week or month from now, "Have you read the book and listened to the tape? How are you doing at applying what you've learned?"

You may come across other resources you'd like to use, but always build a time commitment and an accountability system into your personal growth plan.

The second reflection of the gold sword is vital to understanding yourself and your mate. This one concept alone often brings more instant harmony and team spirit to a family than anything else we teach.

2. UNDERSTANDING AND APPRECIATING A PERSON'S NATURAL STRENGTHS

In our book *The Two Sides of Love*, we wrote in detail about four basic personality types that people tend to exhibit. Some people demonstrate one type primarily, while others are a fairly balanced blend of all four types.

Many excellent personality tests are available today. (We'll mention several in the advanced training section.) But however you choose to measure it, the important thing is to take the time to clearly understand who you are as a person, and who your spouse and children are by God-given design.

Our good friend Chuck Swindoll taught us the meaning behind the familiar verse "Train up a child in the way he should go..."[6] It actually reads in Hebrew, "Train up a child according to his bent." And at our seminars, we've seen a deeper understanding of a child's or spouse's God-given tendencies revolutionize a relationship and dramatically reduce friction in a home.

Such understanding not only helps us to appreciate others' basic strengths, but it can also be a great way to raise our own sense of worth.

At a recent seminar, a man attended who is in charge of a large corporation in Texas. He told us afterward that when he heard this section on personality strengths, he saw himself in a way he hadn't in nearly 50 years.

Our friend has a strong sense of wanting things to be in order and perfectly put together—his house neat, his company running by the book, his every relationship in line. But at times, he has seen his strong desire cause friction with others, even making them feel uncomfortable around him.

After a time, he began to feel he was "different" or had some kind of problem. That made it easier to simply smile and be silent instead of entering into a new situation or conversation. Yet after going through the material we teach, he felt as if a huge weight had been lifted off his shoulders.

As he saw his personal strengths more clearly, he could accept himself better. He *did* have valuable traits that made him an important asset to his family and others. What's more, he realized his weaknesses were really those same strengths pushed too far out of balance! It wasn't wrong to want to be orderly, and understanding that helped him tremendously. But so did the knowledge that his unbalanced strengths could be frustrating and irritating to others.

Differences are cute in a courtship, but they can become irritating and even explosive in a marriage.

Perhaps you've been reacting to your spouse's or child's differences, not respecting them. You're a spender ... she's a saver. You like to eat out ... she likes to stay home. You're spontaneous ... she's predictable. Differences are cute in a courtship, but they can become irritating and even explosive in a marriage. For that reason, this second aspect of the gold sword is extremely important. We highly recommend you go further in depth on this subject by reading *The Two Sides of Love*. In the meantime, the following paragraphs give an overview of the four personality types.

First we have those people we call *lions*. They're take-charge leaders. They're usually the bosses at work, or at least they think they are! They're decisive, bottom-line folks who are doers, not watchers or listeners. They love to solve problems. They're important leaders for any family, office, or church, and they accomplish many great things with their decisiveness and strength of character.

Unfortunately, if they're not careful, they can cause problems just so they'll have something to solve! If their strengths are pushed out of balance, they can be viewed by others as harsh, demanding, dominating, and pushy.

Second are those we call *beavers*. Beavers have a strong need to do things "right" and "by the book." In fact, they're the kind of people who actually read instruction manuals! They like charts and organization. And they're great at providing quality control for a home or business.

Beavers have deep feelings for those they love. But because they want to control their feelings, they often hold back at communicating verbally the softness and warmth they feel. A key part of any team or family, they have great strength in follow-through and detail. But these same strengths, when pushed to an extreme, can make them seem rigid, cold, or perfectionistic.

A third group is our *otter* friends. Otters are excitable, fun-seeking, cheerleader types who love to yak, yak, yak. They're great at motivating others and need to be in an environment where they get to talk and have a vote on major decisions. Otters' outgoing nature makes them great networkers; usually they know people who know people who know people! The only problem is, they usually don't know everyone's name! They can be soft and encouraging to others as well (unless under pressure, when they tend to use their verbal skills to attack).

But because of their strong desire to be liked, they can often fail to deal with problems ("Oh, it'll all work out") and so cause further problems. If they push their strengths out of balance, they can be viewed by others as manipulative, too talkative, poor decision makers, or too changeable.

Finally come the *golden retrievers*. These people are a good deal like their counterparts in nature. If you could pick one word to describe them, it would be *loyalty*. They're so loyal, in fact, that they can absorb the most emotional punishment in relationships—and still stay strongly committed. They're great listeners, empathizers, and warm encouragers.

They also tend to be pleasers who, like the otter, can have great difficulty in confronting or disciplining when necessary. When using their strengths too much, they can be viewed as indecisive, "yes" people, conformers, or afraid of change.

As you can see, with all these animals running around in families, churches, and offices, life can be like a zoo! That's why it's so important that we understand our spouses and children and how their personality strengths blend with others or are different from our own.

If you chose this important aspect of healthy relationships to be a part of your family constitution, we have the following suggestions for your AIT program:

Advanced Individual Training in Understanding Your Family's Unique Personality Strengths

Summary statement of this section:

Understanding your own and your loved one's personal strengths can be a tremendous help in gaining intimacy, increasing self-worth, and overcoming weaknesses.

Self-evaluation:

Rate how you've done with your spouse in relation to this aspect of the gold sword:

I have a clear understanding of my spouse's personality strengths:

(not clear) 1   2   3   4   5   6   7   (very clear)

I can see value in our differences and how they can make us a better team:

(see little value)   1   2   3   4   5   6   7   (highly value)

Sample affirmation statement:

I have come to see the great value of my mate's and children's unique personalities. And I love seeing how all of us blend together into a functional, happy family.

Your affirmation:

_____

_____

_____

Personal written plan:

As a couple, write out your personal plan in this area:

_____

_____

_____

_____

_____

_____

RESOURCES FOR DISCOVERING
YOUR PERSONAL STRENGTHS

Books

Gary Smalley and John Trent, *The Two Sides of Love* (Colorado Springs, Col.: Focus on the Family, 1990). This book goes into greater detail on how to understand your basic personality strengths and how to balance "hard" and "soft" traits in a close-knit home.

Audio and video tapes

"Homes of Honor," session 1 in the video, "Discovering Your Unique Personality Strengths."

In all the thousands of successful homes we've seen, the next area is always at the top of the list of priorities.

3. DEVELOPING MEANINGFUL COMMUNICATION

We are more and more aware that any mutually satisfying marriage must have some kind of regular, meaningful communication. When we do our seminar, we often ask audience members to state the primary thing they think could improve their marriages. Instantly, most people will say, "We need to have more or better communication in our home."

As leaders, men, it's our responsibility to find out how much communication our mates and children need on a daily basis. In interviewing successful families across the country, most say they need about 1 hour of meaningful conversation each day. That doesn't mean an hour straight. Perhaps it's 5 minutes in the morning, a 10-minute phone call from work, 20 minutes at dinner, and another 25 minutes carved out of the evening to provide this much-needed aspect of intimacy.

If understanding personality differences decreases friction in a home, meaningful communication can lower it even further. After a period of drought, it's like a spring shower to a marriage. Arguments often exist because someone doesn't have all the facts. Charge can lead to counter-charge, and soon a simple conversation can turn into a battle. But a battlefield can turn into a place of growth if we take the time to communicate correctly.

There are dozens of communication methods we could mention. (See the last part of this section for more resources.) But for our purposes here, we'll summarize just three of our favorites that produce immediate results: quick listening, emotional word pictures, and resolving.

Quick listening is a simple, honoring method of carefully hearing what your spouse is saying, then clarifying what she said in an attempt to better understand the meaning behind the words. She says two or three sentences only, and then you repeat back in different words what you heard. After you both agree about what was said, you can go back and forth until you've talked through the subject.

Quick listening actually slows down a conversation so that you're forced to really listen to your loved one without reinterpreting what she's saying or "thinking" you know what she means. This process builds lasting respect and cuts down on heated, unnecessary arguments.

A battlefield can turn into a place of growth if we take the time to communicate correctly.

Not long ago, Norma and I (Gary) were asked to give a person a gift of money. When we first talked about this opportunity, I threw out the dollar amount I felt we should provide, and Norma reacted negatively. When she said what she wanted to give, *I* reacted negatively.

Without intending to, we began to argue about this issue. But neither of us had a full understanding of what the other person thought and felt. That's when we slowed down, counted to ten, and started over. This time, we used quick listening to really hear the other person and understand the whys of what each of us had said.

Soon we saw that both of us had valid reasons behind our thoughts, and we quickly came to a solution that honored our feelings and our friend.

For more than 20 years, we've been working at slowing down our conversation whenever friction begins to mount, concentrating on asking honoring questions to find out all the facts and feelings of the other person. And it still amazes me how much that commitment to honor each other in our conversations has enabled us to understand and value each other better.

A second communication method we often use is *emotional word pictures*. Here we take a thought and link it with a story or object that can grab the emotions. This leads to greater clarity and impact than everyday words.

Take writing this book, for example. In many ways, a writing partnership mirrors a marriage. With so many decisions to make on what to put in or leave out of a book, clear communication is a must. And since we're human, there have been times when we've miscommunicated on an idea or story. The important thing, however, is that we're both committed to working the issue through until we finally bring clarity and resolution to the problem. We did just that recently with a single word picture.

Before I (Gary) went out of town not long ago, we had only a few minutes to sit down and talk through the direction of a particular chapter. I thought I had clearly communicated the slant I wanted it to take, and John thought he had carefully heard me. But as it turned out, we miscommunicated, and three days of writing close to our deadline went in the wrong direction.

All kinds of problems could have arisen from that miscommunication. But by using one emotional word picture, we were able to see instantly what the problem was and to move from tension to resolution. Let me explain.

For years, I've had a burden to write this book for men. As John and I talked, I explained that in my mind, this particular chapter was like a 12-story, steel-and-glass skyscraper. Now, I knew John also had a deep burden for this book and chapter, and he's a talented "architect." Yet when I returned, what he had written was like an 8-story, award-winning adobe office building. (Remember, we live in Arizona, where adobe is an art form!)

As we talked about glass skyscrapers and adobe office buildings, we both began to see more clearly what kind of "building" we really wanted to put up in this particular chapter. Instead of one person having to be "wrong" or our differing views becoming irreconcilable, we "painted" the problem with a positive word picture, quickly talked through and moved to a building design we both liked, and pounded out 30 pages in 1 day (which, for authors, is moving out)!

That's the power of an emotional word picture. We've seen people get raises from their bosses; motivate a spouse to go into a stop-smoking clinic; enjoy dramatic improvement in a child's attitude. We've even seen a child bring a prodigal parent back home using this biblical, powerful method of communication.[7]

A third communication method is simply known as *resolving*. It involves taking a single piece of paper and drawing a line from top to bottom, right in the middle of the page. A couple can then sit together, talk about an important decision or issue, and write down the "Advantages" on one side of the page and the "Disadvantages" on the other. Or they can put his feelings on one side and hers on the other. More than any other, this simple method has helped us stay in harmony when talking about sensitive issues.

These are just three communication methods you can use. The important thing is to make the commitment to build great communication in your home, and then learn and practice whatever technique or skill it takes to get there. For more help in this area, go through the suggestions in the advanced training section.

ADVANCED INDIVIDUAL TRAINING IN MEANINGFUL COMMUNICATION

Summary statement of this section:

Meaningful communication is to a marriage what water is to a plant. Sharing feelings, needs, schedules, problems, opportunities, and prayer requests is essential.

Self-evaluation:

Most couples or families know how they're doing when it comes to communicating. Take time here to rate the amount and depth of communication taking place from your point of view.

	Little time				Much time		
Amount of time communicating	1	2	3	4	5	6	7

	"Weather report"			Feelings/needs/plans			
Level of communication	1	2	3	4	5	6	7

Then ask each other in an honoring way, "What would it take to improve our communication level?" After discussing the question at length, write out your own communication plan. You may wish to do that after you've read or listened to some of the resources mentioned at the end of this section.

Affirmation statement:

A possible affirmation statement would be, **"It's natural for me to share my thoughts and feelings with my spouse."**

Write a one-sentence affirmation statement that captures your goal for this area:

_____

_____

_____

The Hidden Value of a Man

Personal written plan:

If meaningful communication is to be part of your family constitution, write out in contract form what meaningful communication *means* to each of you, as well as *how* and *when* it would best take place.

_____

_____

_____

_____

_____

_____

_____

_____

RESOURCES ON MEANINGFUL COMMUNICATION

Books

Gary Smalley and John Trent, *The Language of Love* (Colorado Springs, Col.: Focus on the Family, 1988). In this book, we explain the most powerful method of communicating we've ever seen: emotional word pictures. The greatest speakers throughout history have used them, and they fill the Scriptures. Word pictures can help any family grow in this important area.

For information on quick listening, see our book *Love Is a Decision*, chapter 9 (Dallas: Word, 1990).

Audio and video tapes

Communication is covered in session 4 of the "Homes of Honor" study program.

You've now seen three reflections of the gold sword that can help a man bless his family in ways that will reverberate down through generations. The sooner you start to apply them, the sooner your loved ones will begin to love the difference. But there are four other aspects as well, and we'll look at them in the next chapter. The first of them, if it's not a consistent part of carrying your gold sword, can tear your family apart.

CHAPTER 6

SEVEN REFLECTIONS
OF THE GOLD SWORD

PART 2

We've seen how honor, respecting differences, and meaningful communication can be clear reflections of a man's gold sword. But of all the reflections, this fourth one holds the most promise for positive benefits for your family—and potential for its destruction.

4. DEALING WITH ANGER IN A TIMELY, HEALTHY WAY

The fourth characteristic that makes up the gold sword is the ability to deal with anger in our relationships. Many men fail to see the incredible damage anger does. In addition, they often miss the benefits that come when they deal with anger in a healthy way.

In close-knit relationships, friction is inevitable. Often, that anger comes out of a blocked goal or an unmet expectation, or as a fear-based response. Other times, it comes out of a rightful sense of reaction to wrong.

Ephesians tells us that all anger isn't wrong: "Be angry, and yet do not sin; do not let the sun go down on your anger."[1] In other Scriptures, we're told that even God was angry about sin and hardheartedness. But while the emotion itself isn't wrong, there are definite limits to our expression of it and a strong command that we resolve the dispute in as short a time as possible.

Using the gold sword demands that we deal with our anger. That includes "more-acceptable" forms of anger like a rough tone of voice, slamming doors, or lying by saying, with the blood vessels in our neck about to burst, "Angry? I'm not angry!"

How damaging is anger? Why should we work so hard to rid our homes of its dark side? Try just a few reasons on for size.

Anger increases our stress level, including raising our blood pressure and heart rate.

Unresolved anger has been directly related to higher susceptibility to sickness, serious illness, higher cholesterol levels, rheumatoid arthritis, and even cancer.[2]

Unhealthy anger has been directly related to pessimism and lack of success in the work place.[3]

If anger continues to reside in your heart or that of your loved one, don't assume it will simply get better over time.

Anger changes the electrical patterns in our bodies and brains, forcing many bodily functions to go on alert status or to begin to shut down, awaiting a "fight."[4]

Anger lowers our feelings of self-worth and increases our feeling of being a victim.

Anger opens the door to greater temptation.

Anger puts distance in a relationship and sabotages attempts at closeness.

Anger turned inward can result in symptoms of clinical depression in as little as six weeks.[5]

Anger causes us to be insensitive to the feelings of others as we become absorbed with our own feelings or need for revenge.

Anger pushes us into spiritual darkness.

These reflections of anger catch only a handful of the huge list of negative effects attached to unhealthy, unresolved anger.

No wonder God commands us to begin instantly to draw anger out of our relationships and our own lives! Usually, by being soft, genuinely seeking to understand what happened, admitting when we're wrong, and specifically asking for forgiveness, we can see anger begin to drain away quickly. But if anger continues to reside in your heart or that of your loved one, don't assume it will simply get better over time. Like starting a fire in a trash can in an upstairs bed-room and then leaving the house, you may come back to just a few ashes at the bottom of the can—or to the ruins of an entire house. (Chap. 13 can be an important resource for those struggling with anger.)

Some time ago, I (Gary) was reminded of this when I attended a school reunion with friends from out of state. A close friend from high school days was there. I love and appreciate him, but he was carrying around a massive amount of anger toward his daughter.

Jim had been through some tough times in the past 5 years. First came an angry divorce from his wife of nearly 15 years. Then he watched his beautiful teenage daughter react in anger to both of them and to God by taking on an immoral, faithless life-style. She eventually reaped the consequences of that life-style: She became pregnant out of wedlock and jumped into an ill-advised mar-riage.

After all that hurt, Jim finally turned his life back to Christ. But he failed to give up one thing: his deep anger toward his daughter.

When I saw Jim, he was at an after-reunion party that his daughter had been invited to as well. She had come with her little two-year-old in tow, and Jim had done everything he could to ignore them.

Outside, I talked with his daughter. She wept as she described her feelings of rejection. From her perspective, at least she had married, was thinking of return-ing to school, and was trying to be a good parent—even to the point of rethink-ing her strained relationship with Christ. She was trying to improve her life-style, but she felt her father wasn't accepting her efforts.

There is no emotional hurt like the grief a child can bring a parent. Certainly Jim was hurt. And from a scriptural standpoint, he wasn't wrong in being angry about her rebellion and blatantly sinful attitude. But after two years of her trying to change and grow, he wasn't standing on principle any longer, but on vindictiveness.

He didn't want to forgive her. To release her. To allow her to make a new start. Cutting her off was at least one way he could deal back to her a small part of the hurt she had caused him. I finally had a face-to-face talk with Jim and confronted him about the massive anger he still held toward his daughter. At first he was defensive, even angry at me for bringing up the subject. But slowly he began to see that the goal of discipline in the Scriptures was always to lead those who strayed back to repentance and restoration.[6] And by his anger, he was keeping both himself and her locked in darkness, draining away the very energy and motivation she needed to make positive steps toward loving her husband,

71

her child, and God.

It's not easy to forgive. Jim wanted to see that she was acting normally and fully "functional" before he forgave her and accepted her back with a hug or a verbalized expression of love. And the same went for her child, his only grandson.

I reminded him that by not loving her, he was actually contributing to her dysfunctional behavior. He could still express love for her while being clear that he didn't accept her behavior. He agreed that if God had waited for *him* to be perfect, he'd still be waiting for a relationship with Him. He also agreed that he would show his daughter unconditional love and let the Lord lead her into "normal" behavior.

It may feel good to exercise the kind of power that shuts people off, makes them crawl an extra mile and then another before we'll accept them back again. But it's not God's best, nor is it honoring to Him. If we're serious about carrying the gold sword, we've got to deal with anger in a timely, healthy way.

How to Handle Anger

Here are some ways to rid ourselves and others of anger:

When We're Angry

1. Admit we're usually trying to use something or someone for personal gain.

2. Increase our understanding of what's behind another person's offensive ways. Usually the offender is tired, hungry, or angry himself. The more we see why another is offensive, the less we interpret his behavior as a personal attack.

3. Be ready to forgive others as God has forgiven us. Their attacks on us are like one toothpick in their eyes, but we have many toothpicks glued together in our own eyes (our offenses toward God and others, for which He has forgiven us).[7]

When We've Offended Others

1. Remember that gentleness turns away anger.[8]

2. Increase our understanding of how they feel.

3. Admit our part in the offense.

4. Seek their forgiveness, and wait for a response.

5. Tenderly touch and thank them for their forgiveness.

Honor. Understanding and valuing differences. Meaningful communication. Dealing with anger quickly and healthily. These are all important aspects of our gold sword. And a fifth is every bit as crucial.

ADVANCED TRAINING IN DEALING HEALTHILY WITH ANGER

Summary statement of this section:
Dealing with anger in a healthy way is a crucial part of walking in the light, freeing myself and others to live healthy lives, and restoring relationships to their full potential.

Self-evaluation:
While it may not be easy to admit, we need to evaluate how we're doing at ridding our lives and our loved ones' of anger. Take a moment to do a self-evaluation in this area:

	Great deal					Very little	
Degree of anger I hold toward others	1	2	3	4	5	6	7
Anger others hold toward me	1	2	3	4	5	6	7
Anger I hold toward my own past mistakes	1	2	3	4	5	6	7

Affirmation statement:
When times of anger come into our relationship, I make a decision to listen more instead of reacting—to say words that will be remembered for a lifetime as helpful, not critical.
(Or your own affirmation statement)

_____

_____

_____

_____

_____

Personal written plan:

If dealing with anger in a healthy way is a part of your own family constitution, write out with your spouse your desire and plan for doing that.

_____

_____

_____

_____

_____

_____

_____

_____

_____

_____

_____

RESOURCES FOR DEALING WITH ANGER

Books

Gary Smalley, _Joy That Lasts_ (Grand Rapids, Mich.: Zondervan, 1986).
Gary Smalley, _The Key to Your Child's Heart_ (Dallas: Word, 1987), chapter 1.

Audio and video tapes

"Homes of Honor." Session 5 covers dealing with anger in a constructive way.

The fifth aspect of the gold sword—nonsexual, meaningful touching—is something we have heard hundreds of women across the country say is right near the top of their list of honoring acts.

5. MEANINGFUL TOUCHING

Physical touch is often withheld by men until they suddenly turn "touchie" because it's time, in their minds, to be sexually involved. However, many of these men receive a stiff-arm instead of a warm embrace from their wives. Why?

The average woman needs time to warm up to the sexual experience, in some cases taking as long as two days before she's ready to respond! Her desire grows as she is hugged or touched without sexual connotations attached; as she is praised, encouraged, and helped with things important to her. If a man has supplied these warm-up touches and actions, in most cases he will meet with a warm response from his wife.

As the leaders in our homes, we need to find out how our wives like to be touched, how often, when, and where.

Does your wife want to be touched by you to comfort her when she's hurting?

Does she appreciate an encouraging hug that says, "You can do it! I believe in you"?

Does holding her hand in public provide a great source of security and blessing to her, or would she rather you just sit near her on the couch after the kids have gone to bed and watch a favorite television show?

Men do have testosterone-driven sexual desires that need to be expressed regularly in the marriage. The Scriptures are clear that regular sexual involvement is crucial not only to enrich the marriage, but also to protect a couple from temptation and sexual sin. However, quoting Bible verses to our wives about

As the leaders in our homes, we need to find out how our wives like to be touched, how often, when, and where.

how they aren't to "deny" us usually isn't helpful in increasing a woman's sexual response. Again, a woman needs to be treated with honor, respect, and warmth, and then she is almost always ready to respond. (If not, she may have been damaged by some man in her past—most often her father—something we'll discuss in chap. 9.)

A good friend of ours offered a great example of this to us—and the whole nation! Several years ago, I (John) was on a national television show with Norm Evans, a former professional football player who wears two Super Bowl rings from his years with the Miami Dolphins. During that interview, Norm gave a word picture his wife had used with him that totally turned around their sexual relationship.

While Norm and Bobbie get along great overall, for a time he struggled with her lack of sexual responsiveness. He came home from practice one day and gave her the following word picture. "Bobbie," he said, his voice tinged with frustration, "do you know how I feel about our sexual relationship?"

"Well, I've got an idea. But why don't you tell me?"

"I feel as if every night, we're playing the shell game. Remember that? It's the one with three shells that look the same, upside down on the dresser, and underneath one of the shells is a bean.

"If that 'bean' represents your being sexually responsive, I feel that when I leave the house in the morning, I think I know which shell it's under. But while I'm gone all day, you switch around the shells on the counter, and then when I ask you to become physically involved, you say, 'Pick a shell.' And I seldom pick the right one!

"What I want to know is, when are you going to put three beans under those shells or quit switching them around?"

Norm knew how powerful word pictures can be, and he was convinced that if she didn't immediately throw herself at him, at least she'd be convicted enough that things would change dramatically. But he forgot that two can play at word pictures.

"Norm," Bobbie asked, "would you like to know *why* we're playing the shell game so often?"

"Sure," said Norm. "Tell me."

"Pretend that I'm your favorite fishing rod and reel." Instantly she had Norm's attention, because he loves to fish. "When we were first married, in terms of my sexual responsiveness to you, did I cast well?"

"Well, sure," he said, not knowing where she was going with her story.

"That's right. But over all these years, if I'm your rod and reel, it's as if you've fished me in saltwater time and again, and you've never once washed me off with the hose. And now, because you've never taken care of me, the line is all frayed and backlashed, and the eyelets on the pole are all bent, the tip is cracked, and rust has made the crank really hard to turn. So now, when you try to cast me, all you get is backlash and problems, right?"

"Right!" said Norm, beginning to see the picture.

"Norm, you've spent little time oiling or cleaning or putting on new line. You just toss me in the garage and leave me in the dark, and then you wonder why I'm so hard to cast! *That's* why we're playing the shell game!"

Norm got the picture. He was also wise enough to do what we've been encouraging each of you to do at the end of each of these seven sections. He asked Bobbie directly, "Honey, are you saying that if I learned how to maintain the rod and reel and kept it in really good working shape, you'd put three beans under those shells?"

"Absolutely!" said Bobbie.

"All right!" said Norm, ready to take notes. "So tell me what it means to you to have me put oil on the reel!"

"Okay," she said. "Oiling the reel for me would mean that when you come in the door at night, you don't immediately head to the television set. Come and find me, ask how my day went, and then really listen to me. Maybe even hug me or sit and hold my hand while we talk. *That's* what putting oil on the reel would be like."

"I can do that!" said Norm, finally getting the picture. They went on to talk about "washing off the saltwater," which might be playing with the kids. Other

Emotional bonding comes in the hundreds of "little" things we do with another person.

ways of "repairing the line" might be helping with the dishes or helping the kids with their schoolwork, their baths, or getting ready for bed, school, or even church. (Why is it that some men feel they're only responsible for getting themselves ready for church each Sunday, and then they sit in the car and beep the horn to hurry everyone up?)

Without understanding it fully, we've been told by numerous women that seeing "Daddy" playing happily with the children can actually arouse their passions for their husbands!

On and on their discussion went about a topic that would normally have led to a major argument. But from that night on, Norm and Bobbie had a deeper understanding of and respect for each other than they ever thought possible. Norm finally realized that if he wanted his wife to respond physically, he needed to work at a growing, healthy relationship.

Need more motivation, especially with your children? A recent study of children born in 1951 showed this irrefutable fact: Those children who grew up in homes where they were regularly hugged and touched by Mom and Dad have been both more happy and more successful in life than those who were not.

ADVANCED TRAINING IN PROVIDING MEANINGFUL TOUCH

Summary statement of this section:
Meaningful touching is an important way of expressing warmth and security to a loved one. It puts action to our words of affection and both physically and emotionally blesses those who are touched.

Self-evaluation:
Evaluate how you're doing at providing this important aspect of a growing relationship.

	Rarely provide it					Regularly do	
Provide meaningful touch to my spouse	1	2	3	4	5	6	7
Provide meaningful touch to my children	1	2	3	4	5	6	7

There can be a number of reasons why people resist meaningful touch: national backgrounds and customs, growing up in a home with distance instead of closeness, sexual trauma in the past, unresolved anger, and so on. If you sense a major block to reaching out and touching your loved ones, chapter 13 will be an important resource for you.

Affirmation statement:
I am excited to provide, each day, the level of meaningful touch that my wife and children need to really know and see my love for them.
(Or your own affirmation statement)

_____

_____

_____

_____

_____

_____

_____

Personal written plan:
If this aspect is part of your marriage and family plan, take time to talk about what types of touch are needed in your home, how often they're needed, and when they are most effective and appropriate.

_____

_____

_____

_____

_____

_____

Take a large dose of nonsexual touching and add it to honoring, valuing differences, dealing with anger, and meaningful communication, and you've got a nearly complete picture of the gold sword. But two final concepts provide its full reflection and point of thrust.

6. REGULAR EMOTIONAL BONDING EXPERIENCES

C.S. Lewis pointed out that deep friendships only come "in the context of doing something else together." In other words, genuine friendship comes from doing something more than just sitting around talking about friendship. It's in taking weekend trips together, planning mini-vacations, going on dates, or even walking or jogging together that a close bond is built.

Emotional bonding comes in the hundreds of "little" things we do with another person; they usually become the biggest factors in building a really satisfying relationship.

Surprisingly, rough times can bond us the closest. Time and again, those who have gone through significant times of crisis together have kept that bond for years. Just go to a gathering of war veterans and you'll see it. The camaraderie forged on the battlefield remains strong through the years.

As men, we need to realize that we can't spend all our time golfing with our business partners, watching sports with our neighbors, and escaping out of town with our clients and then expect to bond with our wives or children. It takes commitment to carve out time to pray and play together, exercise together, enjoy each other, and laugh with each other. But the closeness that results is worth it.

Recently, our (the Smalley) family took its last vacation together as a family of five. Within a few months, both my oldest son and daughter will marry, and soon we'll have a son-in-law and daughter-in-law added to every family picture. Already, we're talking about going camping with our yet-to-be-born grandchildren, and Norma and I can hardly wait. Why? Not because we like bugs and leaves falling in our food, but because time spent together in a meaningful activity can bring a level of emotional bonding you'll never get any other way.

From a walk in the park to that once-in-a-lifetime trip to Hawaii, look for ways you and your loved ones can experience positive times together.

ADVANCED TRAINING IN EMOTIONAL BONDING EXPERIENCES

Summary statement of this section:

Emotional bonding times are experiences we provide for our spouses and children that form the basis of positive memories. Whether we take a walk in the park or a trip to Australia, and regardless of whether it rains on our picnic or our flights are canceled, sharing meaningful experiences is a great way to increase positive family feelings.

Self-evaluation:

Rate how you're doing at providing the kind of bonding experiences your spouse and family will remember in the years to come.

	Rarely provide it					Consistently	
Provide bonding times with my spouse	1	2	3	4	5	6	7
Provide bonding times with the children	1	2	3	4	5	6	7

Affirmation statement:

We regularly schedule time to be together as a family. And when things go wrong, we count that as an opportunity to get closer together!

(Or your own affirmation statement)

_____

_____

_____

_____

Personal written plan:

If you decide to add emotional bonding experiences to your family constitution, talk through what types of experiences—from small to large—would help your family move forward as never before. The results of this discussion, put in contract form, could be written here.

_____

_____

_____

_____

_____

_____

RESOURCES ON EMOTIONAL BONDING EXPERIENCES

Books

Gary Smalley, _The Key to Your Child's Heart_ (Dallas: Word, 1987).
Gary Smalley and John Trent, _Love Is a Decision_ (Dallas: Word, 1989).

Video and audio tapes

"Homes of Honor." Emotional bonding is covered in section 6 of this study program.

As we pointed out earlier, one clear aspect of honoring our loved ones is providing security for them. While many things can add to the security a spouse or child feels, one major source of _in_security is financial irresponsibility.

7. FINANCIAL STEWARDSHIP

Consider what happened in Mike's family. He continually complained that their finances just weren't working out each month. He'd moan and groan about how tight things were in the budget, and he'd blow up if his wife made a purchase at the grocery store without using a coupon. _Then she discovered a box full of hobby supplies he had hidden that had cost hundreds of dollars._

Mike talked responsibility, but he didn't live it, financially or otherwise. And if there's anything that instantly snaps our gold sword, it's dishonesty in handling our money. Many times in counseling, the problem that brings a couple in is a crisis over a mate cheating on taxes and getting caught, or one overspending a clothing allowance to look good and axing necessities.

As far as women are concerned, financial accountability is an important aspect of our carrying the gold sword. If we're really to be the leaders in our homes, then as head stewards and supporters, we need to be faithful in this area.

Of course, a wife's undisciplined behavior can also lead a couple to financial ruin. While many families today need the second income a wife can provide, it's also true that many women have entered the work force looking for some kind of "inner fulfillment" or to afford the payment on a house they just have to have. What's often overlooked in this second case is what's best for the children who are farmed out to day-care centers that have great-sounding names—and often little else that's great for the kids trapped there.

Additionally, some women can put tremendous pressure on a man to earn a certain standard of living. Almost nothing puts more strain on a relationship than a man working his hardest for a paycheck, only to have his wife belittle his efforts as not fulfilling her expectations.

I (John) have a long-time acquaintance whose wife typifies this. Mark is a cabinetmaker, and a good one. He built a small company and works extremely hard at his craft—even harder at pleasing his wife. With his every step up the ladder, she has demanded he stretch out two steps in debt. A new van. A larger

As far as women are concerned, financial accountability is an important aspect of our carrying the gold sword.

house. A still-larger house with horse privileges.

I ran into Mark one day at a local convenience store. He's a physically strong man. But you could tell by his eyes that he'd been crying. Why? Because he'd had to sell most of his tools to keep his new house away from the bank one more month. Some of those tools his father had given him, and the rest he'd collected over a lifetime. And to top things off, he had to tell his two young daughters they wouldn't be going back next year to the Christian school they loved.

Most women aren't like Mark's wife. They look for ways to save money, not spend it, and appreciate our efforts in the financial area. God has more than answered my prayers with Cindy, my wife of nearly 15 years. She came from a background where finances were often scarce if construction jobs ran out, and six people shared a two-bedroom apartment—with one bathroom.

Never once has Cindy put financial pressure on me. She could see that I was willing to work hard, and she is also thankful for small things as well as large ones. That's been a tremendous blessing in my life.

Financial faithfulness is a key element of carrying the golden sword, providing the kind of home that honors God. Our goal is that of the proverb writer: "I don't have so much that I forget you, O Lord, nor so little that I am forced to steal and dishonor Thy Name."[9]

There's so much we'd like to say in this area that someday we may write our own book about finances. But our good friends Larry Burkett and Ron Blue are already doing an excellent job of writing about the financial basics, and we recommend you pick up the books mentioned in the advanced training section. However, before sending you there, we have to address one financial principle that we've seen make or break far too many homes. It's something I (Gary) had to face head-on in our home.

After ten years of marriage, Norma and I had accumulated a sizable amount of debt. Credit cards. Gas cards. Student loans. Car loans. A house loan. Added up, it began to spell potential trouble for us if we didn't get a handle on it. And that began a two-year process of paying off all our bills by cutting back, cutting out, and paying only cash in every situation we could.

We endured 2 years of sacrifice until we had our own "break even" party when we finally were debt-free. That was 20 years ago. And since then, we've lived on a cash basis as much as possible. In addition, Norma has worked for the past 8 years as the administrator of our ministry (and her own boss), which gave her an income, but also the flexibility of schedule to be wherever the kids needed her to be (like home after school, attending their events, etc.). We've both worked hard to stay out of debt, and while it may take you 2 months, 2 years, or 10 years, the emotional and financial freedom it brings makes it that much easier to concentrate on carrying the gold sword.

ADVANCED TRAINING IN FINANCIAL FAITHFULNESS

Before you move on to the next chapter, we urge you to finish this important exercise.

Summary statement of this section:
Financial faithfulness involves taking an active role in managing the resources God has provided for present needs, as well as prayerfully creating a clear plan for the future.

Self-evaluation:
When it comes to financial stewardship, how do you see yourself doing with today's resources and with preparing for a secure future?

	Weak management					Strong management	
Financial stewardship today	1	2	3	4	5	6	7

	No plan					Clear plan	
Financial plan for tomorrow	1	2	3	4	5	6	7

Personal written plan:
If financial faithfulness makes up a part of your family constitution, write out in contract form what a good "financial plan" would look like for both of you.

_____

_____

_____

RESOURCES FOR FINANCIAL FAITHFULNESS

Books
Larry Burkett, *Your Finances in Changing Times* (Chicago: Moody, 1982).
Ron Blue, *Master Your Money* (Nashville: Nelson, 1986).
Ron and Judy Blue, *Raising Money-Smart Kids* (Nashville: Oliver-Nelson, 1988).

BUT IF MY GOLD SWORD IS SO IMPORTANT, WHY DO I STILL STRUGGLE TO PICK IT UP?

We've now seen seven reflections of the gold sword and a long list of reasons (in the previous chapters) why we need to wield it expertly. But if picking up the gold sword is so critical, why don't more of us do it more often?

Why do we hesitate?

In all our research and counseling, we consistently see things in men from coast to coast that hold them back. The first is their lack of knowledge of the incredible power that comes from joining their swords with those of others in a "gold sword" group. The benefits, motivation, and encouragement that men get from joining with other men are staggering—so much so that we've listed just eight incredible benefits in a "must read" chapter (chap. 12, "The Hidden Power of Friends"). The message of that chapter is so important that we considered placing it next, just to make sure you got to it as quickly as possible. You may still want to turn to it right now. For some of us, however, our reasons for not picking up the gold sword are described in the five short chapters that follow. They list five "roadblocks" that can stop a man cold from picking up or using his sword.

Did you realize that right within your brain is something that can make it difficult for you to reach for the gold sword? Were you aware that there's one force within us so powerful that it can rip the gold sword from our hands? Are you living with a woman who has faced a silver swordsman in her past and who hides your gold sword when you try to use it today? Was something left out of your past that makes your task of carrying the gold sword five times more difficult than that of other men who didn't experience this loss? Have you been trying to keep something intact that only enriches your life when it's broken?

In the next five chapters, you'll find the answers to those questions. But we urge you to remember that just beyond these roadblocks are the solutions that can lift you above them. From the massive support of a circle of gold swords in chapter 12, to the one-on-one coaching that can help to heal a broken past in chapter 13, to a look at the Master Swordsman Himself in chapter 14, help is coming.

As you read on and face the first roadblock to gold swordsmanship, you'll see what every man carries within himself that can make the sword almost too heavy to pick up.

A Reminder to Our Readers

This section covers several of the major roadblocks we see affecting men nationwide. One or more may be something you're directly facing or that you can see in a close friend.

However, as important as understanding these hindrances is, be sure you read on to the solutions. Beginning in chapter 12, "The Hidden Power of Friends," you'll begin to see how you can gain incredible power to overcome these or other roadblocks.

CHAPTER 7

BEING MALE MAY BE HAZARDOUS TO YOUR FAMILY'S HEALTH

"**I** know I need to pick up my gold sword, but it doesn't come naturally. I don't think about it the way my wife does. I just don't seem to be wired to carry a gold sword!"

At many seminars and in a number of counseling sessions, we've heard words like those. And while some men might hide behind them as an excuse for not being warm and relational, *the words hold a measure of truth for most males.* As science discovers more about how our brains are "wired" differently as men and women, there is mounting evidence for innate gender differences. Some of them directly affect our initial, natural desire to pick up the gold sword.

A DECISION, NOT A FEELING

Some critics might say that certain aspects of personal power we've described in this book are just not natural to men. When it comes to initiating gold-sword actions, men are not inclined toward the verbal, nurturing, touching, tender, one-on-one, encouraging side of life. What comes easily to the average woman often seems to be a genuine struggle for men.

These words might sound like heresy in an era when the feminist movement speaks with such militancy in denying any significant differences between the sexes (beyond the obvious physical ones). Yet the facts are mounting against the feminist assertion that male and female differences are simply cultural rather than biological.

89

Men and women are equal in value before God, *but we are very different.* And these differences, science is discovering, exist from the time of conception. Reports from the laboratories of leading brain scientists on both sides of the Atlantic reveal strong reasons why men gravitate to the silver sword rather than the gold.

In their landmark book, *Sex and the Brain,*[1] researchers Jo Durden-Smith and Diane deSimone chart recent scientific discoveries that have revolutionized the way the scientific community views the inherent differences between men and women.

Studies by research psychologist Diane McGuinness indicate that the portion of the brain called the *hypothalamus* controls the body's flow of sex hormones, and these hormones govern the differences between male and female behavior.

Men and women are equal in value before God, but we are very different.

"Some of these differences appear extremely early in life," writes Dr. McGuinness, "and others are more obvious after puberty. But the fascinating thing is that they seem to be independent of culture—as true in Ghana, Scotland and New Zealand as they are in America."

To what kind of differences is this researcher referring? She goes on to say, "Put in general terms, women are communicators and men are takers of action.... Males are good at tasks that require visual-spatial skills, and females are good at tasks that require language ability. Males are better at maps, mazes and math; at rotating objects in their minds and locating three-dimensional objects in two-dimensional representations. They're better at perceiving and manipulating objects in space. And they're better at orienting themselves in space. They have a good sense of direction.

"Females, on the other hand, excel in areas that men are weak in, especially in areas where language is involved.... They're better at almost all the skills that involve words: fluency, for example, verbal reasoning, written prose and reading—males outnumber females three to one in remedial reading classes. A woman's verbal memory is also better."

Some feminists claim that all this can be explained away by cultural expectations and conditioning, but that simply doesn't wash in the face of research. From *infancy*, boys are attracted to three-dimensional objects, lights, and patterns. They are always curious about their physical environment and begin exploring as soon as they're able to crawl. When a boy is old enough to draw pictures, he immediately begins sketching various *objects*.

Baby girls, however, respond differently. "Girls respond preferentially to the people in their environment," Dr. McGuinness notes. "What is catching for them are *faces* rather than objects. They are also much more sensitive to sound than boys are. And they respond to the social sounds around them, to tones of voice and music.... It is almost certainly an important contributor to the female's early developing verbal abilities. Sounds and people are remembered, as against objects in space. Communication versus action and manipulation. There is evidence to support the idea that tendencies in these directions are present in the male and female brain from the beginning."

The researcher's conclusions are unmistakable. "These things are not culturally induced. They're biological. Just as the capacity for language is pre-wired into our brains before birth... so, in females, is a special skill in it.... What comes easy to either sex is likely to be biologically programmed, like the hypothalamus: stamped, primed, waiting to be developed."[2]

Even a recent issue of *Time* magazine, not known to carry the banner for conservative causes, featured the front-cover story "Why Are Men and Women Different?" The subtitle read, "It isn't just upbringing. New studies show they are born that way."[3]

BECOMING MORE A MAN, NOT LESS

What does this mean when it comes to our holding and using the gold sword? Have we just made a case, citing a man's natural wiring, against everything we've said so far about a man's need to be relational, warm, and encouraging? Are we trying to make men into something other than what God designed them to be? to make them something *less* than the natural man?

Not less ... *more*.

As believers, we never were called to be "natural" men but spiritual men— men of God who have a lower (human) nature but a higher calling. (Just read Rom. 7 to see the struggle Paul faced with his natural tendencies to use only the silver sword.)

Without a doubt, it's traditional for men to define their lives relative to their ability with the silver sword.

It's traditional for men to leave the gold sword hanging like a dusty moose head over the mantle.

It's traditional for men to say, "It's my job to clothe and feed them. It's their mother's job to make them feel loved."

But if it's easier for a man to pick up the silver sword than the gold one ... well, nobody ever said life was easy, especially the Christian life. We can't walk away from the clear challenge God gives us that can draw us higher than "tradition" and cause us to rely on His supernatural strength rather than what's natural.

Two Crucial Challenges

Men have always been hunters, warriors, and adventurers. The call of a challenge—whether it's picking up a sword to join the Crusades, setting sail in a small boat across the Atlantic, or tackling a Mount Everest "because it's there"—is something God has wired within a man.

And without question, God clearly lays a challenge before us to pick up the gold sword. This is not an easy challenge, perhaps not even a natural one, but it's one we can't shrug off or avoid.

It's not natural to exercise, but we need to do it at least three times a week. It's not natural to eat well, but it makes no sense to end up with a hundred-thousand-dollar estate and a ten-dollar body at retirement. It's not natural to pick up our Bibles or turn to the Lord in prayer, but we bring leanness to our souls if we don't.

One strength of a man is that he responds to what *isn't easy*—to challenges and hills to climb and oceans to conquer ... and a gold sword to pick up.

Paul made that clear in his letter to the Thessalonian church. Although he was speaking about his own ministry style while in Thessalonica, his words have a direct application to men in the context of a family. The apostle wrote:

"For you know that we dealt with each of you as a father deals with his own children, encouraging, comforting and urging you to live lives worthy of God, who calls you into his kingdom and glory."[4]

Some ten years later, Paul urged the Colossians (men included) to "clothe yourselves with compassion, kindness, humility, gentleness and patience.... [T]each and admonish one another with all wisdom."[5]

God's Word simply expects—commands—men to use their personal power, to pick up the gold sword. While we carry a silver sword, we're also to add tenderness, patience, comfort, and encouragement with our wives and children, just as our heavenly Father does with us.

And what happens when we do make the extra effort to pick up a sword that may not be natural for us? Whenever a man chooses to let the warmth of his gold sword radiate through his home, *it triples in power*. It opens eyes. Pulls back shades. Causes a stir. In some instances, it is virtually unforgettable.

I (John) remember playing my heart out for a high school football coach who rarely (I actually thought never!) used his gold sword to encourage or praise. It was late in a game we were supposed to win, but we were losing. And

When a man makes an effort to pick up the gold sword and use it under God's control, the world takes note.

while I thought I had played a good game, in the fourth quarter I was pulled out after making a tackle.

Here it comes! I thought to myself as I jogged up to the coach. As the captain of the defense, I was going to get blasted for losing the game and benched. But that's not what happened.

"John," he told me, "I just wanted you to know that I wish I had ten more of you out on the field. I'm proud of how you played tonight. Now get back into the game."

It has been more than 20 years since I nearly fell down after hearing his words. I remember floating back onto the field and playing even harder than before. We lost the game, but I won something that never showed up on the scoreboard—a crystal clear picture in my mind. I had the lasting memory of a silver sword expert who picked up the gold sword just one time with me ... and made 4 years of effort seem worthwhile.

Men tend to remember for decades specific words of encouragement their fathers spoke to them. When a man makes an effort to pick up the gold sword and use it under God's control, the world takes note. Women and children certainly take note. And the more we pick it up, the more we will shape those who love us and look to us to help define their lives.

Scripture encourages us to be strategic in the use of our words. When we speak, let's make our words count for something! Let's use words that build and encourage rather than tear down or demean.

As the apostle Paul said in Ephesians 4: "Do not let any unwholesome talk come out of your mouths, but only what is helpful for building others up according to their needs, that it may benefit those who listen."[6]

Solomon said, "A word aptly spoken is like apples of gold in settings of silver. Like an earring of gold or an ornament of fine gold is a wise man's rebuke to a listening ear."[7]

Let your words be like gold, men of the golden sword! Let your words be like a finely crafted piece of 24-carat gold dropped into a life that's ready to receive it. You don't have to speak all the time; just make sure your words count! Here are some suggestions:

- A timely compliment to a discouraged mate.
- A firm but loving word of warning to a wandering adolescent.
- A big heaping of praise to a child who is trying so very hard to please you.
- An upbeat, confident appraisal of a situation when "the facts" are frowning another message.
- Words of trust and praise in the Lord God.
- The words "I love you" anytime.

Men of the golden sword, let your words be golden! Let the moments with your family be golden! Let your touch be golden!

It may not be natural for us, but it's right. And with God's power, it's a challenge we can't afford to pass up.

This first roadblock can get in our way as we seek to use our personal power, or it can loosen our grip on the gold sword. However, *the roadblock in the next chapter can rip it right out of our hands for the rest of our lives.*

Read on and see what we mean.

CHAPTER 8

THE LITTLE "E" CAN SPELL BIG TROUBLE

I n the next few pages of this book, you will encounter your greatest roadblock to picking up the gold sword. How you confront this issue will determine whether that sword lights up your home, guards your wife and children against dark intruders, and leads your family into all the wonders God has for you ... or ends up as an unused relic that finally lands on a garage sale card table, stuck between a Vegematic and a pet rock.

In my own life, I (Gary) first caught sight of this serious roadblock, "the little 'e' for ego," after I'd been married less than two years. The realization came like an abrupt punch in the stomach; it left me gasping for air.

I was sitting in a marriage seminar when some curtained portion of my mind was suddenly jerked open. The speaker had been talking about how a husband and wife need to respond to one another's physical and emotional needs. In one chilling instant, I realized that 100 percent of my sexual energies had been devoted to figuring out ways for my wife to stimulate, please, and satisfy *me*, my ego.

It had never occurred to me that she might have sexual needs and desires, too. I just assumed she must need the same things I did. I had never thought to ask her about it or to look for reasons why she didn't feel sexually responsive to me at times.

Instead, if she frustrated my desires at all, I would become instantly angry. I would jerk myself over to my side of the bed and lay there with my back toward her, alone and brooding. I didn't even want her feet to touch mine. And when she would reach out to me in the darkness and say, "Gary, don't you want to talk?" I would pull away and tell her to leave me alone.

It had been like that since our honeymoon. Either she performed according to my expectations or I would slam the door on any communication at all.

I don't know how much of the seminar I heard the rest of that day. I guess I'd heard more than enough. My mind was blown open to the fact that most of my life had been centered on myself. For the first time (but not the last), I realized just how self-centered a man I am. I remember getting alone by the couch that night after Norma went to bed and falling on my knees. I confessed to God that I was the most self-centered person I knew, but that with His help I wanted to spend the rest of my life finding out how to meet my wife's emotional and physical needs.

I determined to back off trying to satisfy my own desires for a while, and to wait on God to reveal Himself and His ways to me. In the meantime, I did everything I could to focus on Norma's needs and wants.

Several weeks later, she grabbed my arm and looked me right in the eyes. "You haven't mentioned sex in three weeks," she said, "and I need to know what's wrong. Don't I appeal to you anymore? Have I done something to offend you?"

"No," I said with a smile. "I just want to concentrate on meeting your needs ... for a change."

As Norma realized I was serious, an amazing thing began to happen in our bedroom. The more I focused on trying to please and satisfy her, the more I found my own needs fulfilled. We were both experiencing more joy and satisfaction in our sexual relations than we ever had before.

I was reminded of the Lord's words that "whoever wants to save his life will lose it, but whoever loses his life for me will find it."[1] If you give up your life—or any part of it—for the sake of Christ, He always finds ways to give it back to you. You lose what you try to grab for and hold on to. You get back what you give up. It was a pleasant surprise for me as a young man to discover that the Lord's faithfulness to this principle held true even in my sex life.

For me (John), the reality of my self-centeredness also came at the expense of my wife—and our pocketbook. I was driving a ten-year-old car that was begging to be sent to the junk heap when suddenly the "car bug" hit me like never before. I'm not sure exactly what planted the idea in my brain, but suddenly there was only one thing to do about my car situation.

I detested the sticker shock that went with buying a new car, so I was determined to do something "smart." I'd buy a classic car that would gain value the minute I bought it instead of losing money on a new car the second it was driven off the lot.

What was the answer to my personal car quest? Only one vehicle—a shiny red 1967 Ford Mustang. Cindy describes my behavior then as being on a car "hunt," not car shopping. When I finally found just the car I wanted, I bought it on the spot.

I never took seriously the repeated warnings of my wife that it was impractical and "not what I'd really like." I brushed aside comments from friends that you really had to hunt to find a "restored" car that didn't need major restoration. I was as blind and self-centered as I've ever been ... and I learned my lesson the hard way.

If you give up your life—or any part of it— for the sake of Christ, He always finds ways to give it back to you.

Within a few weeks, I had engine trouble, which became major engine overhaul trouble. Then I made the mistake of taking my "bargain" to a good friend who owns a body shop ... and having him point out all the clever ways the new red paint job had covered over the need for several new panels, and even a new hood!

In the following weeks, the blinders finally came off, and I realized I'd bought a major project for which I paid not only with hard-earned cash, but also with insensitivity to my wife, disregard of my friends' counsel, and a huge dose of selfishness.

Self-centeredness is a major negative emotion that can push the gold sword out of reach. For this reason, some men never do feel the power of that sword in their hands. Others of us hold the sword for a while and then feel it slip away.

Have you ever been using an electric Weed Eater or hedge trimmer when you walk beyond the range of your cord? Suddenly you're disconnected. Without power. You can't accomplish anything. Suddenly that helpful tool in your hand becomes useless; it's just a hunk of metal and plastic.

That's what happens to the gold sword of personal power when we become preoccupied with ourselves. The golden light of its blade fades away. The power drains out in an instant. The once-productive, powerful sword becomes a useless, dead thing in our hands—just a dull hunk of metal.

Could that be why you're having trouble wielding the gold sword in your home? in your church? in your business? Could you have inadvertently "unplugged" it by drifting into self-preoccupation?

If you have, try what I (Gary) do when I've faced the reality of my own self-centeredness. Make an honest list of all the expectations you've been carrying around. Take a blank sheet of paper and write them out. Start with a few general categories like work, recreation, food, people, travel, and ministry, and list specifics under each.

As you examine your list, think about how you long for those people, things, and situations to somehow cooperate with you, bring you fulfillment, and fill your empty cup. That's a normal, human characteristic. And yet it blocks your ability to carry the gold sword. It produces the very things you don't want to see in your life: anger, fear, worry, bitterness, frustration, and depression. These manifestations of a self-centered nature are right at the heart of sin and all that opposes God.

THE TWO BIGGEST SWORD-STEALERS

What draws out our self-centeredness as men? In the two stories above, you've seen the two biggest sword-stealers most men face. The first may come with a red paint job and drive a man into the red as a result. It's our preoccupation with toys as boys ... and more-expensive toys as men.

Where do you see this type of selfishness? Try the Super Bowl. The TV advertising rates for a Super Bowl separate the corporate men from the boys. The tab for the most recent gridiron extravaganza came to something over $800,000 a *minute*. For that kind of currency, the Madison Avenue gurus are expected to provide some pretty high-powered slogans, tunes, and jingles.

So when the Reebok athletic shoe company flashed its slogan before the millions of Super Bowl viewers, it hit on a proverb that cuts to the heart of our times: "Life is short. Play hard."

In other words, have fun. Go fast. Pile up toys. Increase your pleasure. Do it *now*.

Financial pressures to appear more prosperous than our neighbors can claim a huge bite of our time and energy. Beyond our God-given responsibilities to provide food, clothing, and shelter for our families, it's easy to chase after the silver sword to somehow "prove ourselves" to our friends and peers. To many men, it becomes vitally important what kind of ink pen they carry, what kind of watch they wear, what kind of boat they tow behind what kind of car, and so on and so on. Things, things, things. But remember, life is short, so play hard.

We're working so long to buy our toys (or ignoring our families in our "hunt" for them), however, that what's really important in our homes slips out the back door while we're not looking. If we want to be men of the gold sword, we can't close our eyes a moment to the danger of these pressures to "buy, buy, buy." Messages of "material fulfillment" literally saturate our society and will leave us with an empty sheath the moment we drop our guard.

> *It's difficult for even good men to be unaffected by the sexually charged atmosphere of our times. Today, Sodom is a satellite dish.*

If that "lust of the eyes" we've been describing doesn't get us to become self-centered and drop our swords, we face an even more powerful sword-stealer: the "lust of the flesh."

Sexual pressures have shaped men since God first invented testosterone in His lab. From the beginning of time, the sight of a beautiful woman has been enough to lay kindling on the fire that always smolders within a healthy man.

In the latter half of the twentieth century, however, society has been spraying jet fuel on those fires. The fumes of it fill the atmosphere, the clothing stores, the airwaves, the schools and universities, the printing presses, and even the "900" phone lines. The result has been a raging fire storm of harassment, rape, sodomy, incest, abuse, abortion, blasted homes, shattered lives, and deadly diseases. The perpetrators are mostly men; the victims are mostly women and children. Even though tens of thousands are dying in these flames, our world responds by spraying more and more jet fuel.

It's difficult for even good men to be unaffected by the sexually charged atmosphere of our times. Abraham's nephew Lot got himself and his family in trouble because he pitched his tent too near the gates of Sodom. Today, Sodom is a satellite dish. It pitches its electronic tent in far too many homes.

Even if we manage to flee adultery, sexual pressures still threaten to steal the sword of our personal power by pushing us into self-centeredness. We get lured away by "soft" pornography (low-octane jet fuel?), mental fantasies, masturbation, and asking our wives to do things that offend them. Before long, we find ourselves singing the same refrain as the rest of our sensual culture: "Stimulate me. Turn me on. I want to use you. I want you to fulfill me. I need to be satisfied."

According to Ephesians 5, the more of this kind of thinking we indulge in, the more we lose the edge on our gold swords. Soon, the blade of our lives becomes so dull that we have virtually zero impact on anyone for Christ. We might as well be flaying about with an ostrich feather.

Solomon's counsel in the book of Proverbs has incredible application for a man who wants to hang on to his gold sword in the face of today's high octane sexual pressures: "Above all else, guard your heart, for it is the wellspring of life."[2]

In the end, it takes the power of God Himself to enable us to guard these fickle hearts of ours from self-centered sexual temptation. If it's infinitely more difficult for men to lead pure lives in these times of ours compared to previous centuries, then we have infinitely more need to be on our knees before a faithful, all-powerful God.

FACING SELF-CENTEREDNESS BEGINS WITH AN ADMISSION

The key to overcoming self-centeredness in any area of life is to first recognize it and admit it! I (Gary) could not carry the gold sword into the sexual area of my marriage until I understood how deeply I had tainted it with my self-serving demands. I couldn't use the gold sword in my early ministry until I admitted that one big reason I had even gotten into it was to feed my ego and "prove something" about myself. The fact is, none of us can do much of anything with our personal power until we face up to our deeply rooted selfish motives and turn away from them with all the strength God supplies.

But then ... then the gold sword becomes a singing sword, and life is filled with its music.

History shows that at the beginning of every major revival, there has been a fresh realization of mankind's self-centered ways. When people finally understand how deeply they're concerned about pleasing themselves and how little they care about pleasing God, they begin to fall on their knees in repentance and seek each other's forgiveness. Almost immediately they go to their brothers and sisters, people in their churches, people in their neighborhoods and towns, and seek reconciliation. It's such a stunning, supernatural turn of events that it pierces to the heart of any community. And then the dam breaks, releasing a great torrent of God's grace and power.

It's time for a group of bold men to say, "I've had enough of this love affair with myself. I'm going to repent. I'm going to swim against this irresponsible, playboy current of my culture. I'm going to stoop down low and pick up the gold sword. Even if no one else does it, I'm going to do it anyway. It has to start somewhere, so let it start with me. I'll admit it. I am self-centered. I want to confess that to God and to you. Will You forgive me, Lord? Will you forgive me, my wife, my children?"

Will you be one of those men?

If you will, we guarantee that no one will find a tarnished gold sword with your name on it in a garage sale.

We've been playing around as a nation for more than 40 years, and we men have been leading the charge. As homes splinter, crime and violence soar, women and children turn away from us in disgust or distrust, and our national prestige sinks to new lows, it's time for us to stop being playboys and find the gold swords we've lost or forgotten.

That won't happen, however, if we loosen our grip on our swords by ignoring our natural tendencies, or if they're ripped out of our hands by self-centeredness. And there's a third roadblock that can leave us swordless, too—the type of women who hide a man's gold sword. Turn to the next chapter and meet these women.

CHAPTER 9

WOMEN WHO HIDE OUR SWORDS

I magine coming home from one of our seminars, fired up about being the leader of your home. You've had your eyes opened about learning how to love, and you've vowed to pick up that gold sword in your home if it's the last thing you do.

Yes! you tell yourself. *I can do this!* You're excited. You're motivated. You're going to conquer this thing and join with thousands of men around the country in a "circle of gold swords."

As you listened to our teaching in these areas during the seminar, you thought of ways to have a sexual encounter with your wife that's really going to be meaningful to her for a change. A couple of days after you get home, you give it a try.

You've done the right things. You've talked to her during the day. You've been personal. You've offered affection and security. You've even told her you love her—right out loud. You've hugged her several times during the day in an affirming, nonsexual way. You think to yourself, *I've got this down. I've been doing everything Smalley and Trent were telling me to do. It's been gold sword all the way. This is going to be a great night!*

Finally your wife is getting ready for bed. You slip into the bathroom and slap on a little wild musk cologne. You've already agreed with her earlier that tonight's going to be the night. You crawl into bed with her, get close, and ... she totally freezes. You're in bed with a plastic mannequin.

103

It begins to dawn on you that nothing—a capital N *Nothing*—is going to happen tonight. And you can't believe it.

You react. She reacts. You think, *Wait a minute. I've done all the right things. She even said tonight was gonna be the night!*

Now she tears up and starts crying.

You say, "What's wrong?"

She says, "I don't know."

You feel as if she has taken your gold sword and smacked you over the head with it. "Women!" you say. "I suppose it's 'that' time of month or something."

"I don't like you bringing that up!"

"Well, I can see that pimple on your face. So it must be that time, or close to it. I can't believe women!"

That comment elicits a volley of angry words and results in an even colder shoulder.

Your hormones have been pumping throughout your body, and you were about as excited as you can get ... and now you're about as frustrated as you can get.

Why is she reacting this way? Why has she grabbed the gold sword out of your hands and run you through with it? Why do women sometimes take a man's gold sword and hide it somewhere, just as he discovers it and begins to learn how to handle it?

There are four main reasons. Before this chapter is complete, you will understand why you might have a surprise sword fight on your hands, with a determined foe.

Why do some women react this way?

1. BECAUSE THEY'VE BEEN VICTIMS

We may not realize what our wives are going through. They may not realize it. But if a woman has been abused as a girl by one of her parents—especially her father—she will still be responding to that trauma, no matter how many years in the past it occurred, unless she has received help. If her father was an alcoholic, was angry or distant, rejected her, committed incest with her, or walked out on the family, chances are that man is going to be sleeping between you and your wife. No wonder you feel distance! No wonder you can't reach her!

A woman who was abused and has not found healing or restoration may begin to sabotage her relationship with you in a number of ways. For example, let's say your wife was hurt deeply by a significant man in her past. Maybe it's a father who treated her cruelly. Maybe it's an older brother or uncle who molested her. Maybe it's a boyfriend who raped her on a date or a former husband who was unfaithful. If she has not worked through her anger, if it's still smoldering, red and sullen, in the depths of her soul, she will be unable to bond with you in the way that part of her really wants to.

Anger produces low self-esteem. A victim feels that low self-esteem deeply. As a result, while she longs for affection, she can actually resist being treated with tenderness or consideration. Because she isn't used to seeing the gold sword (or if she's been the only one carrying it and bonding with the children as a result), she can feel threatened and actually resent your newfound sensitivity.

If a woman is really locked into the pain of the past, she may provoke you any way she can to treat her in a dishonoring way. Why? Because feeling alone or rejected, as bad as it is, is more familiar and seems more fitting than feeling loved or unconditionally accepted. Unfortunately, her "comfort zone" is one of negative emotional reactions, not positive ones. What a terrible tragedy!

This is all very frustrating and discouraging to a man who is trying to make a fresh start as a husband and do all "the right things" to honor and value his wife. He's got that gold sword in his hand, and it's shining with all its beauty and brilliance in his home, but his wife just can't seem to respond.

If that's the case in your family, your wife needs the same solutions for her problems that you need for yours. These sorts of problems will not go away if you leave them alone. They won't disappear naturally. As I (John) often say in counseling about a couple's problems, "Remember, more of the same won't bring change." If the problems *do* change on their own, it will usually be for the worse.

To create healthy growth in this area, both of you can use the practical suggestions in chapters 12 through 14. So don't give up. Help is on the way.

Why do women try to hide our gold swords? There's a second reason.

2. BECAUSE OF NATURAL TENDENCIES WITHIN WOMEN

We've seen that men have a number of natural tendencies. What about women? Let's consider a few of the traits they naturally evidence.

A. *Because of their superior abilities in building meaningful relationships, women may make light of our attempts to use our personal power.*

Most women grow up speaking the language of the gold sword. It's instinctive. Intuitive. They're actually born prewired for it. For that reason, we men can appear sort of dense in these areas, a little slow on the draw. Women sometimes expect us to instantly comprehend things we simply don't understand. They see us stumbling around, avoiding issues, and chasing silver-sword goals, and it makes them angry. So they begin attacking and criticizing us.

I (Gary) try to explain this to women in our seminars by telling a story. Suppose I find myself lost in a major American city, and (as a last resort for many of us men) I pull over to the curb, roll down the car window, and ask a dignified-looking, middle-aged man if he can give me some directions.

But instead of answering, the man looks at me and then keeps walking down the sidewalk!

Frustrated, I pull forward a little and ask him again. But he just stops, brushes a piece of lint off his lapel, and doesn't say a thing.

By this time, I'm getting angry, and I begin to raise my voice. "What's wrong with you, mister? Are you deaf? Why are you treating me like this? That's not the way we treat people in Arizona! In case you haven't realized it, I'm a stranger in your city, I'm lost, and I just need a few simple answers. Now are you going to help me or not?"

This time he looks at me, gives a little bow, opens his mouth, and replies in polite Italian. Then it dawns on me that this guy doesn't speak a word of

If a woman has been abused as a girl by one of her parents—especially her father— she will still be responding to that trauma, no matter how many years in the past it occurred, unless she has received help.

English!

At this point I ask the ladies in the audience, "Would it be insensitive of me to stay angry with that man for not answering my questions and helping me find my way? How many of you think it would be insensitive?" (I ask for a show of hands, and of course 99% of the women raise their hands.)

It *would* be insensitive to remain angry with this person. But then I say to them, "Do you know that's just the kind of thing you women do to us men? We don't speak your language! We never learned to speak the language of the gold sword. We don't understand all the subtleties of your relational way of living. Yet you think we do.

"So you look at us with one of those 250,000 facial expressions you can make as a woman, put your hand on your hip, and say things like, 'When are you going to get with the program!' Many men do not have a clue to the program! Nor do we have the same interests. Nor do we have the same preprogrammed ability with the gold sword. Yet you expect us to act and comprehend and respond as if we understood everything."

As men, we are extremely sensitive about feeling inadequate. One of our deepest needs is to feel adequate. Competent. The Bible calls it "respected."[1] Yet without realizing it, women can make us feel terribly inept when it comes to relationships. And even when we get motivated to try our hand at using the

Most women grow up speaking the language of the gold sword. For that reason, we men can appear sort of dense in these areas.

gold sword, some women may mock or disregard our bumbling, heavy-handed attempts.

Until we begin to "get in practice" with our gold swords, until we get the feel and the heft of that marvelous blade in our hands, we may simply have to endure some misunderstanding. We may not receive the strokes and encouragement we would like to get for making ourselves vulnerable and stepping out into this risky terrain. That's why we need the encouragement of other men in a small group until our wives realize we're serious about making strides and taking leadership in this crucial area of life.

B. *Some women naturally tend to hide our swords during their physical cycle.*

When I (Gary) was younger, I had the hardest time remembering this aspect of "living with my wife in an understanding way."[2] On several days each month, I'd find myself married to a strange woman! She was critical, irritable, and always hovering near tears. It just didn't make sense to me. She would take me apart for what seemed to me the most innocent of infractions—things I'd been getting away with all month. Then suddenly, *blam!* I was "insensitive, rude, crude, gross, and heartless." Inevitably, we would get into some kind of conflict, and then she would become really upset.

About that time I would hit myself on the head and say, "Wait a minute! This must be that time of the month. Hey, this isn't a *real* fight, honey. It's just hormones!" But all that great insight earned me was another night in the cooler.

We men have to realize that because of the chemical changes a woman goes through in her monthly cycle, there are certain days of the month when no amount of gold swordsmanship will impress her. She can knock the sword right out of our hands. But we can ask her questions like, "What are some of the best ways I can make it through those days? Maybe we can do some special sword polishing during those times."

C. A *third natural tendency of certain women could simply be labeled "personality makeup."*

In our book *The Two Sides of Love*, we explain the different personality types in detail. One combination we call a "lion-beaver." That's the kind of person who not only says, "There's one right way!" but also, "It's my way!" If a woman has this personality bent, she may be a strong leader and a perfectionist wrapped into one. Inevitably, these women seem to marry men who exhibit what we call the "golden retriever" temperament.

Men who reflect retriever characteristics are faithful, loyal, friendly, and tend to be more sensitive and relational than many other men. The strong-minded woman can blast the gold sword right out of her husband's grip by being too heavy-handed, too critical, too nit-picky, or too overbearing.

But that's no time for a man to give up! The gold sword remains extremely powerful. It will make a difference in our most important relationships. It will transform our homes. But it may take time. It may take counseling. And it will almost certainly take the encouragement and support of other men around us as we meet in the "circle of gold swords" we'll describe in chapter 12.

Why do women seek to hide our gold swords?

3. BECAUSE THEIR SPIRITS MAY BE CLOSED BY ANGER

Contrary to what you might think, one of the most important things a man can do each night before bedtime is not locking the doors and turning out the lights. It has more to do with *un*locking doors and turning *on* lights.

Unresolved anger in your home is more toxic than the radon gas that seeps up from the earth and threatens many houses across the country. Radon has become such a fashionable environmental threat that hardware stores have cashed in by selling detection kits.

If only there were an "Anger Detection Kit"! If a man, by his actions, words, or neglect, has caused anger in the hearts of his children or wife during the previous 24 hours, if he has closed their spirits and caused them to draw away from him,[3] it's critical for him to deal with those situations immediately. Anger that is sealed up or allowed to fester turns into the worst kind of relational poison.

As we have already written, when anger coats a relationship, the gold sword is turned aside. It can't penetrate. It's tarnished and blunted. Yes, there will always be a certain amount of anger in any normal home, but as Scripture counsels, it must be dealt with before the sun goes down.

Why do women hide our swords?

4. BECAUSE OF THE FALL

After the fall of Adam and Eve in the book of Genesis, God confronted them with the consequences of their disobedience. "To the woman he said, 'I will greatly increase your pains in childbearing; with pain you will give birth to children. Your desire will be for your husband, and he will rule over you.'"[4]

Many commentators who have wrestled with the original Hebrew language through the years have interpreted that passage to mean the woman would continually try to rule over the man. In her human nature, in her knee-jerk reaction to a million life situations, she would be faced with a constant temptation to take control and exercise authority over her husband. This really comes out of a woman's self-centeredness, just as we explained a man's self-centeredness in chapter 8.

The remedy is the same as we offered to men: becoming aware of this tendency toward self-centeredness; confessing it; repenting; experiencing revival in your heart; and then making sure you concentrate on the principles and suggestions in chapters 12 through 14, especially 12. Chapter 12 is a key to solving this problem of a woman's natural tendency to take over and ram through her own agenda.

Sometimes, however, a woman's desire to take over is perfectly understandable. She sees her man stumbling around, out of control. She sees him ruining the family, the marriage, his relationships, even his own health. So she reaches out and makes a grab at the situation. She says, "If he's not going to do it, I'm going to do it." There are certainly times—tragic times—when this just has to be done. There are times when a woman must act to protect herself or her children.

The problem occurs when this tendency pops up again and again in the normal operation of the home and family. Women tend to take over when they see us failing or tripping over our gold swords in a given area. And how do we respond?

"Okay, you want that? Fine. Then take it. I've got silver-sword things to worry about anyway." And we back off. If we continue that pattern and slough off relational responsibilities, seldom exercising our God-given personal power,

Women tend to take over when they see us failing or tripping over our gold swords in a given area.

we can do great harm to ourselves, our wives, and our children.

As men, we have to step back and look at each area of struggle objectively: "Okay, as a man, what should I be doing here? My wife wants to take over, but I need to stay involved. I need to take the initiative."

As we wrap up this chapter, I (Gary) can't help but reflect on something that happened recently when John and I were on a national radio talk show. A distraught man phoned in and said his wife had left him. Worse still, she was openly living with another man right in front of the kids. It was grieving him and their children, and he just didn't know what to do about it.

I spoke into my microphone to the lonely voice, somewhere thousands of miles away, through the darkness of that night.

"Let me ask you a question," I said.

"Okay."

"What kind of relationship did your wife have with her dad?" I knew what he was going to say, and he said it.

"Well, her father was an alcoholic. He was very abusive to the mother and kids, and finally he walked out on the family."

I felt like screaming over the radio. For some reason, I'd had it that day.

"You know," I began disgustedly, "I am just about up to my neck with stories of how men are treating women. Especially fathers with their daughters. It makes me want to throw up. Do you see what's happening here? Here's a woman who has been abused by her dad, and now she's unable to love her husband. She's now destroying her relationship with her children—losing their respect forever—and she's continuing the cycle of sins visited on children and children's children by a messed up, godless father."

The other end of the line was silent, and the radio host looked as if maybe he wanted to jump in and move to another caller in Milwaukee or take a station break. I waved him off. I needed to have this say.

"Men—all you men across the country who are listening to this—in God's name, let's bond together. Let's help each other. Let's help the fathers out there.

Unresolved anger in your home is more toxic than the radon gas that seeps up from the earth and threatens many houses across the country.

Let's help the husbands. Let's find a way to put a stop to this terrible negative cycle that's pulling us all downhill."

It's true even in terms of this chapter. If you're living with a woman who can't love you, who can't respond to the gold sword, chances are she never saw that warm glint of gold in her own home. It confuses or intimidates her. She never saw it in her father's hand. So here again (and again and again), it's traceable back to that father. Back to a man.

As men, we ought to stand up to the consequences of our neglect, to our responsibilities, to the truth, and say, "Okay. So we've really messed things up. Is there still room to use a gold sword? What can we do now?"

If we don't pull out our gold swords, families throughout our nation will plunge into ever deeper darkness.

Let's choose a different direction.

Let's walk against the wind of our culture.

Let's endure the opposition, the inconvenience, the sacrifice.

For a change, let's lead the way.

And if we don't?

Then we'll face more roadblocks. Like a fourth that can devastate both us and our families if we don't control it. The next few pages will show how our own past can hinder our ability to use the sword. More importantly, they'll show how we can overcome the effects of that past.

A Reminder to
our Readers

You've looked at three of the five major roadblocks that keep a man from picking up his gold sword. These next two, *overcoming a difficult past* and *choosing honesty above "image management,"* are also important barriers.

But remember, beginning in chapter 12, you'll find the first of three concepts that are essential to carrying the gold sword and overcoming these roadblocks. *If you're in need of some encouragement right now, feel free to skip ahead to chapter 12 and read through to the end of the book. Then you can come back to chapters 10 and 11.* But if you know you struggle with past hurts or overconcern with your "image"—or have friends who do—turn the page to see how those things can hinder your effectiveness with the gold sword.

CHAPTER 10

HEALING THE HOLE IN OUR HEARTS

Eric looked like all the other wrestlers standing around the two large practice mats. He had on the same wrestling sweats. He was lean and wiry and looked as if he went through all the roadwork and training sessions of the other boys his age. But when the coach blew his whistle and had everyone else hit the mats for push-ups, sit-outs, and sit-ups, Eric stood aside.

You see, Eric had a problem. A tiny, almost microscopic hole kept him from the sport he wanted more than anything to take part in. That hole was in his heart, and it kept him a spectator frozen on the sidelines. He could pick up everyone else's towel, but he could never really be a part of the team.

Unfortunately, when it comes to using the gold sword in meaningful relationships, too many men are frozen on the sidelines, just like Eric. They, too, often long to get into the battle and use their swords to carve out a great relationship, but they have holes in their hearts that hold them back—an inner void put there by a painful past that keeps them from being all they can be in the present.

If a man's past includes being rejected by the primary male figure in his life—his father—he can't run away from it. Just as these friends can't...

"When I was eight years old," Sam told us, "I was into building model cars and airplanes. My favorite was a '57 Chevy that I spent hours painting and detailing. It sat on the shelf above my bed, and I wouldn't even let my friends touch it.

"One day, I did something that particularly upset my dad. (I think I had used one of his tools from the shop and forgot to put it away.) He took me outside and made me watch as he poured gasoline over my model and lit it on fire as punishment."

Jerry also experienced a childhood trauma. "My father died when I was four," he said, "and my mother remarried—a man with one son, a year older than me. I loved my stepfather and wanted so much for him to love and accept me.

"My brother, Chris, was an excellent soccer player. He played on 'select' teams and got many awards at different tournaments. I was a band kid, and while I did equally well on band days, I could always see a difference.

"Whenever Chris had a success, the recognition doubled at home: celebration dinners, special-order cakes for the 'winning soccer player,' special privileges for winning a tournament. But on the day when I was voted to the all-state band for my instrument, all I got from my father was a weak 'Good job.'

"I can remember sitting at the dinner table that night, watching my stepfather laugh and joke about soccer with Chris ... and knowing I would never be a real part of his life."

These are just two of hundreds of stories like them that we've heard over the years. They all echo the same message of lasting pain and rejection. And for all those men, emotional trauma as a child dramatically affected their ability to pick up the gold sword as adults.

But every memory of a father doesn't have to be negative. Some people have experienced just the opposite, a level of acceptance that hasn't hidden their gold swords from them or left them without the emotional strength to hold them high.

"My father wasn't perfect," Ben said, "but he seemed that way to me. He didn't become a Christian until late in life, and while he changed a great deal, one thing he just couldn't seem to do was give up smoking.

"One time my father tried to quit but failed. He hid his smoking for several weeks, and we all praised him for his apparent success. Finally, he did something I'll never forget.

"He got everyone in the family together in the living room and had us all sit down. Then he apologized for lying to us and asked our forgiveness. I knew it wasn't easy for him to humble himself or to verbalize that he cared, but that night he told us, 'I'm quitting this habit because each of you means a

116

great deal to me.'

"I can't think of a time when I was prouder of my daddy or more thankful I had him."

Jim told us, "My father died on August 22, 1989. He was the best example of a father I know. He would tell us he loved us any time, any place, in front of anyone.

"One Saturday evening, I had a friend come over to my house to spend the night. As we were walking down the stairs, my dad was just coming home from work, obviously exhausted. Still, when he passed me, he stopped and gave me a hug and said, 'Jim, I love you,' and then walked on upstairs to bed.

"I didn't think anything of it. That was just typical Dad. But my friend was absolutely shocked. His father had never once said that to him.

"At my father's funeral, nearly ten years after my friend witnessed that stairway scene, he told me how much that hug in the hallway had affected his life. And then he told me that I was the luckiest guy in the world to have

If we've grown up with our fathers' acceptance at arm's length, we can easily shove our families away as well.

had a father who loved me so much. He was right!"

A hug in the hallway. Words of encouragement. The courage to admit we've lied in front of our children. These are examples of gold-sword power. And we hope these last two stories were the ones you could most relate to. But we can only visit Disneyland; we can't live there. For some of us, those first two stories of rejection would just be a warm-up to what we've suffered.

If rejection was a consistent part of our past, isn't it enough to just forget it? to push those memories aside every time they come up? to just bury the hatchet? Why dwell on the past? It isn't healthy to spend all our time dwelling on it. And it's fine to bury the hatchet.

But most of us remember exactly where we buried it. And even if we've overcome the inner anger of being rejected or abandoned by our fathers, we're still at risk. That's because *distance* in a primary relationship, like between father and child, does not teach closeness in our future relationships with our spouses and children. If we've grown up with our fathers' acceptance at arm's length, we can easily shove our own families away as well.

If we've come from a hurtful past, we must be willing to face that fact honestly. We've written three other books that go into greater detail on dealing with past hurts (*The Blessing, The Gift of Honor,* and *Joy That Lasts*)—and others have done helpful books as well[1]—but here are two principles that can help heal that hole—and get you on the mat with a winning team.

1. IF WE DIDN'T HAVE GODLY MENTORS GROWING UP, WE NEED TO FIND ONE TODAY!

"'Wake up, Joshua!' my mother would say. 'Your father's coming for you!'"

Our friend Joshua is 88 years old, yet his memories of a loving father are still strikingly vivid.

"There were lots of times when Mom wouldn't have to wake me in the mornings," he told us. "I'd be lying in my bed, smelling the bacon and eggs cooking downstairs, and listening for my father.

"Before he took me out with him to the fields to work, he'd always walk to the barn and hitch up the horses. I can still remember the sound of the team and wagon as it pounded across the bridge on the way to the house, with my father sitting up on the buckboard singing.

"I couldn't wait to sit beside him at the breakfast table and then climb up beside him on the wagon. I didn't realize it at the time, but I was getting daily lessons in what it meant to be a real man."

Joshua experienced what every little boy longs for. There's a deep need within each child to "do what Dad does," and an even deeper longing to learn what a man does.

In Joshua's years on the farm, he got everyday lessons in how to face man-sized challenges. Like the time their only water pump broke and they had to work all night to fix it. Or the time their bull got out and gored a neighbor's horse. Or when Miss Betty down the way accused his father of shorting her on her order of chickens, and his father had to resolve the problem.

By watching his dad at work, Joshua was able to picture his own place in the male world. How to react. What to stand for. What to fight against.

Unfortunately, that rarely happens today. Our super-technology and glass-enclosed workplaces don't cater to children, and they don't build the father-son bond. An average father working 60-plus hours a week will usually do so away from the house, and his work involves matters that are far beyond a child's comprehension.

What's left is for Mother to try to tell the child what Dad does and who he is instead of the boy's getting to view it himself. And what's sacrificed is what boys in an agrarian society had—the shoulder-to-shoulder, side-by-side mentoring of a man.

Structured programs can give a father and son this needed man-to-man exposure—tremendous programs like Scouting, where there are man-to-aspiring-man camping trips and weekend projects. These planned activities are important, even vital. Yet for every man who includes his son in his life, there are a hundred who have no convenient place to fit him in.

"Children aren't allowed past the security gate at work or I'd take him occasionally," a modern father might say. "And I pay professionals to fix things around the house, so that lets that out. Why, even on the golf course, it only slows down the foursome behind us when my son tags along. You know how busy the course gets on weekends."

Logical reasons. But the logical conclusion of excluding our sons from our lives is that they pick up a feminized version of masculinity from Mom or a

The logical conclusion of excluding our sons from our lives is that they pick up a feminized version of masculinity from Mom or a distorted image of manhood from peers.

distorted image of manhood from peers.

The lack of positive mentors today is the first thing missing in most men's hearts. It can create a tiny hole there. Fortunately, it's one of the most solvable problems.

In the Scriptures, God made sure we know we're members of a family. In 1 Timothy, we're told that we have "spiritual fathers" and "spiritual mothers"—even "brothers and sisters"—to relate to. If we missed out on the mentoring process with our fathers, then linking up with a godly model today can be one of the most important things we'll ever do.

It's something both of us have had to do to heal the holes in our own hearts, holes put there by difficult pasts and silver-sword fathers.

The Hidden Value of a Man

For me (John), mentoring came during seminary with my exposure to a master mentor and noted Christian educator, Dr. Howard Hendricks. I can remember my first day of graduate school at Dallas Seminary, sitting in the snack area and hearing a fourth-year student I highly respected say, "I can't believe it! I actually got into Hendricks's discipleship class! I've waited four years for this!"

Waiting four years to get into a class? I didn't believe any course could be that interesting. But I learned later that I had been waiting all my life for what that course taught. Only 12 students were allowed to sign up for a personal "mentoring" class taught by "Prof"—12 students out of more than 500 who may have wanted in. But I knew deep inside that I needed to be there.

I signed up for his class my first year of seminary so I would be able to take it in my fourth year (so long was the waiting list). And when my fourth year finally rolled around—I'll never forget the impact those months of personal involvement with "Prof" had on my life and ministry. In fact, it was through those one-on-one and small-group sessions with Dr. Hendricks that I made up my mind to go into full-time family ministry.

A mentor who helped to heal the hole in my (Gary's) heart was a man named Rod Towes. He loved Christ, the teenagers at my church, and me. He stepped to my side when my father died, and his influence has meant the world to me over the years. At a time when I needed a man's presence the most, Rod would often call me at home. "Hey, Smalley," he'd say. "I've got to go and meet with Norm Wright. How about you come along with me so I don't have to ride alone?"

He made it seem as if I was doing him a favor. But those times with Rod were actually a tremendous blessing to me. Time after time, Rod would take me with him to meet an important pastor or teacher who was his friend.

"Meet my good friend Gary," he'd say. And I'd get to shake hands with another man who was making a vital difference in the Christian community. Those meetings gave me the right kind of heroes—men of strong faith—at an age when boys long for them.

Spending time with Rod at work, at play, with his family, and with our youth group—those were some of the most important teaching times in my life, and they were all accomplished outside a classroom. And still today, I love it when Rod flies into town, comes over to have dinner with my children, and shows them the same love and affection he showed me years ago.

If you've grown up with a hole in your heart as we did, you don't have to stand on the sidelines. Healing can begin with the blessing that an older man in your church, at your work, or in your neighborhood can bring. But there needs to be someone.

In addition to a godly mentor, there's a second factor that's essential to gaining the strength to carry the gold sword.

2. MARK YOUR OWN INNER "RITE OF PASSAGE" THAT CLOSES THE LOOP ON YOUR CHILDHOOD.

Many men who grew up with a hole in their hearts never emotionally grow out of childhood. In many ways, by missing out on the affirmation of a father or other significant male figure, they never "close the loop"[2] on childhood and can remain emotional adolescents. What do we mean by this?

In many American Indian tribes in days gone by, braves went through a "time of testing."[3] In the secular men's movement that's exploding today, much has been made of the various African cultures that provide a male "rite of initiation." Some groups are even replicating parts of these ceremonies, taking father and son into the woods, beating on drums, and marking a change from boyhood to manhood.

While elements of this movement are helpful, what sheds the most light on this genuine area of need is Scripture. In the Old Testament, the "blessing" between father and son is well documented.[4] Providing a living picture of a time of transition, the mantle of leadership was passed from one generation to the next through spoken words and physical touch.

"Come here, my son, and kiss me.... [and] he blessed him."[5] In Genesis 27, 47, 49, and elsewhere, the importance of this blessing is shown clearly. And derived from these traditions, orthodox Jewish homes today still provide a coming-of-age bar mitzvah (and bas mitzvah) to signal the end of childhood and the beginning of adulthood.

But what's so important about a test or ritual when it comes to our manhood?

In our society, there has been a blurring of where youth ends and adulthood begins. Back when we were an agrarian society, a boy had a specific set of skills to master before he was considered a man. Many stories of the early frontier tell of a 14- or 15-year-old whose skill with a gun, axe, or plow had moved him into the ranks of adults. (Billy the Kid was only 14 when he gunned down his first man. Talk about misuse of the silver sword!) But where are the mile-markers today in a son's road to adulthood?

The age of 18 is often when young people are legally considered adults. However, all that age signals today is the beginning of an extended adolescence. For many, years of subsidized college and graduate school lie ahead if they're to become "marketable" and prepared for our high-tech, highly competitive society.

Yet even during this time of extended schooling, there's a deep need in all adolescents to know when they've crossed the line into adulthood. And that need is often ignored in a home that leaves a hole in the heart ... never providing a challenge or test to pass that becomes a milestone marker of maturity.

Unfortunately, this genuine need in a young man's life has been tapped and twisted by the explosion of gangs across our country. In places in our cities where the family structure has broken down, peers become charged with tremendous influence in a young person's life. And for a boy seeking manhood, gangs offer a clear-cut line of male acceptance.

Unfortunately, that line is often drawn in blood.

Here in Phoenix, the police task force on gangs has identified an alarming trend. Boys wanting to join a gang must pass a severe test: They must shoot someone to be considered worthy as gang members.

This test led 2 smiling 12-year-olds to walk up to a woman in her car. Knock on her window. Politely ask her to roll it down. And then fire 7 rounds at her at point-blank range.

The Scriptures confirm a man's basic need to go through an authenticating test or challenge. Dr. Bruce Waltke, an eminent Hebrew scholar, provides tremendous insight into the creation passages in the book of Genesis. Of particular interest to me (John), when I sat in his class, was the crucial importance he placed on what happened *between* the creation of Adam and the presentation of Eve.

Adam's longing and need for Eve came from first accomplishing a significant task—naming all the animals. In doing this massive job, his incompleteness was awakened, and then God fashioned his completer for him.

How does all this apply to men who struggle to fill in the hole in their hearts? In many ways, the men we see in midlife crisis are those who have never had a clear sense of completing an "authenticating task."

That's not to say they haven't earned a high school or college degree. Often, these are men who have worked hard, struggled up the corporate ladder, and achieved outward success. But it hasn't given them a sense of inner completion or rest. And a man who doesn't feel a sense of completion in the tasks he has performed is a man walking toward an emotional cliff.

Take Frank, for example. After eight years of an up-and-down marriage, he finally walked into the emotional no-man's-land of marital separation. In a counseling session he told us, "I'm 42 years old, but I don't think I've ever really felt 'grown up.' I don't think my dad has ever looked at me that way, either.

"He's a working-class guy, and he's never related to anything I've accomplished in my profession. I can remember working so hard to finish my MBA degree. I was 28 at the time and thinking, *This is it! I've finally arrived!*

"But when graduation day came, my father conveniently said he had to go out of town to get the prop on his boat serviced, and it was Mom, again, who was the only one to see me walk across the stage."

To look at Frank's story is to see there was never a time in his life when his father (or that mentor we talked about earlier) said verbally or nonverbal-

A man who doesn't feel a sense of completion in the tasks he has performed is a man walking toward an emotional cliff.

ly, "You've made it! Congratulations! You've crossed the line and have joined me as a man."

His father's indifference to his accomplishments stopped an inner developmental clock that should have moved him toward responsibility and genuine manhood—the gold sword—and instead left him childishly self-absorbed at work and self-destructive in close relationships.

One way to heal this hole in our hearts is to understand our need to close the loop on childhood. The games played and adult toys collected by an adolescent 40-year-old can make him feel as if he has stopped aging, but gold chains and youthful feelings won't fool a clock.

We're not advocating a trip to the woods this weekend to pound drums and cut a notch on a tree as the secular men's movement gurus suggest. But a trip back through your past to see what you've accomplished, making mental marks of key times of growth, is an important step.

For those who have an older son at home, we have a special challenge and question for you. Have you helped close the loop on childhood for your son? Have you taken him to dinner, written him a letter, taken him for a long walk, given him a plaque, or in some other way communicated verbally that he's no longer just your child, but a man in your eyes?[6]

You'd be surprised how powerful such a message can be for someone, even in his forties or fifties, who still lacks the assurance that he has "passed the test"—particularly someone who struggles with the everyday responsibilities it takes to be a man.

We've looked at two factors that can rob us of a sense of significance as men: the lack of a positive role model (father or mentor), and failing to close the loop on childhood. And in chapters 12, 13, and 14, you'll find three more crucial solutions to dealing with a difficult past and getting the gold sword firmly in hand.

In chapter 12, you'll discover the incredible, healing power that comes from a small group of men helping each other hold up the gold sword. It's often here that you can find that mentor and those close friends who can begin to shrink the hole in your heart. In chapter 13, you'll see how one call to a particular type of coach can initiate a process that can help drain away buckets of anger and shrink that hole even further. And finally, in chapter 14, to gain a clean bill of health—and the Great Physician's okay to get back in the battle—we'll look at why a strong relationship with our heavenly Father is just what the doctor ordered.

Next we turn to the last barrier to gold swordsmanship. It's the tendency many of us have to hold up our finish line blue ribbon when we've only made it to the halfway marker. It's talking about being an expert at using the gold sword without ever picking it up. It's going through all the classes and lessons but never having had any hands-on experience.

We can deal with the past. We must. And when we do, we'll be helping to protect ourselves from this last major roadblock.

CHAPTER 11

WHEN ACTIONS DON'T MEASURE UP TO WORDS

Have you ever been hiking or hunting and run out of water? Every year during the spring here in Arizona, we have some winter visitors who drive out into the desert without a canteen. And as their thirst mounts, suddenly, off in the distance, their eyes catch a reflection of something on the horizon. A glint of silver. Something too good to be true. A lake they can just make out. And their hearts begin to pound.

It couldn't be, yet there it is ... gleaming, sparkling in the afternoon sun. Maybe two or three miles away. And aren't those trees—real trees—along the edges? A smile crosses their cracked lips. A man could camp on the shore in some shade, drink his fill, and get refreshed!

So off the trail they go toward that glimmering, shimmering promise on the horizon.

But it never gets any closer.

It's always just ahead.

And then, somehow, they're out of their cars. Face down on the ground. And their mouths are full of dry, dry sand.

"Well," you say, "would anybody actually be that foolish?"

Unfortunately, the answer is yes. Entire families have fallen under the spell of a mirage, only to learn too late that they have been bitterly deceived by a strange atmospheric phenomenon. But stranger still are

men who risk their families chasing the final roadblock we'll look at—
something as empty as Arizona sand.

I (John) know all about this roadblock and its power to lure a man
away from using the gold sword. In a sense, my own father left our family
stranded in a desert as he chased a mirage caused by his silver sword, and
it has taken us years to find our way out.

WHEN OUR PUBLIC AND PRIVATE
SELVES DON'T MATCH UP

Many of us are so fearful of losing positional power and our standing
as silver swordsmen that we would do almost anything to hide our personal failures, weaknesses, and errors in judgment. As a result, we end up living two different lives.

We have a public self, the one everyone sees, and a private self, the
one with all the blemishes, warts, and inconsistencies. Because these two
images don't match up, it takes a great deal of emotional energy to prop
up that outward facade. That's what we call image management.

It feels like power, but it isn't. It's a mirage. And it can kill you.

When my brothers and I were toddlers, my dad still lived at home—at
least he slept there. He would work all day and then go out with his buddies at night. Sundays, however, were an exception. Back in the early
fifties, many people in Phoenix took a stroll down Central Avenue after
church on Sunday afternoons.

All the nice shops were downtown at that time, and Central was the
place to bump into all your friends and neighbors. Dad would be there,
too, pushing us twins in the stroller and leading our older brother by the
hand. We would all be dressed up in our cutest clothes, Dad in his best
suit. For a couple of hours, we would stroll up and down old Central, Dad
smiling, waving, and greeting people.

Why the Sunday devotion to the family? Frankly, it was good for business. As an insurance agent, Dad thought it would help him make contacts if people saw him as a devoted family man with cute little kids. The
rest of the week, however, he didn't want any responsibility for us at all.

My dad wanted two images, and he only kept the public one to
enhance business. He thought that showing off his gold sword would
bring him clients. But since there was no inner character to sustain the

image, it soon collapsed. Within a few months, he gave up trying to maintain appearances and left the family for good.

He was not alone among men who live two lives. Rand Kerry lost everything to the same mirage. It should never have happened. As the publisher of a major newspaper in the Southeast, he should have been able to command all the attention he wanted on the Atlanta cocktail circuit.

His paper was profitable, highly regarded, and featured an array of

Many of us are so fearful of losing positional power and our standing as silver swordsmen that we would do almost anything to hide our personal failures, weaknesses, and errors in judgment.

award-winning reporters, columnists, and cartoonists. That should have been enough to give him confidence at any gathering of the city's prime movers. It should have made him more than comfortable among his peers.

Strangely, it didn't.

Something always rankled when the men began boasting about their war experiences, as men occasionally do after a few drinks. Kerry had nothing to talk about in that department, and it pained him.

Back in 1950, he had wanted to ship out to Korea with some of his college friends, but a 4-F draft classification kept him setting type at a small-town newspaper while his buddies dodged bullets in the frozen Korean hill country. He was ashamed that others were risking their lives for their country while he worked at a safe, quiet job stateside. He carried that shame for years.

Maybe that's why he told the lie at that exclusive dinner party at the Radisson. It was just a small fabrication, but what a sense of power it gave him! He simply told several of the men that he, too, had been in the service.

Kerry was pleasantly surprised with how much mileage that offhand remark brought him. The men actually stopped talking, looked up from their drinks, and appeared interested. He was sure he could detect a new level of respect in their eyes. It only grew when he modestly mentioned his role at the battle of Pork Chop Hill.

Then there was no going back. The mirage had him by the throat. Kerry's years of reading and study about the Korean conflict and his own writer's imagination made the deception easy to maintain ... and enlarge. Further research helped him come up with the right division, company, and platoon numbers. A trip to several surplus stores supplied him with a uniform and battle ribbons. He even found a service medal at a pawn shop. He liked to see it gleam in the light of his reading lamp at his desk. He could have earned it. He *should* have earned it. Sometimes it almost seemed as if he *had* earned it.

Ironically, a blue-chip reporter at Kerry's own newspaper became suspicious, checked on his publisher's background, and discovered he had never been in the service at all! By the time the wire services picked up the story, Rand Kerry's career was over. He not only lost his position and his profession, but he also lost all the legitimate respect he had built up through a long career marked by diligence, talent, and integrity.

Rand Kerry had seen what he thought was a vision of power at that Atlanta dinner party. By the time he discovered it was all a mirage, it was too late. He should have known better.

I (John) should have known better, too. An old Arizona boy like me shouldn't go chasing after mirages. Yet I also once found myself lured into the illusion of image management. As a result, great strain was placed on one of my most important relationships. If I hadn't learned how to let it go, it might have hurt my life and my ministry deeply.

THE COURAGE TO TRADE AN IMAGE FOR HONESTY

A few years ago, Gary and I were in the middle of an earlier book project. We also had several magazine articles due at the same time. Here at Today's Family ministry, Gary often solos on speaking and teaching assignments around the country, while I handle many of the writing chores.

When Gary called me from the East Coast, he seemed particularly concerned about one of the impending magazine deadlines. He had already done his part, and I was supposed to pull it together and send it off.

"How's that article coming along?" he asked.

I knew I would be working late that evening, that before I went to bed (if I went to bed), the article would be done. I also knew Gary would be upset if I told him it wasn't done yet. A deep concern of his is the value we place on our commitments to publishers, and because I gave him my word it would be completed, I had to make sure I followed through. Besides, he might also think his associate in ministry wasn't as competent, tireless, disciplined, and efficient as I wanted him to think!

So I lied.

"It's done, Gary," I said.

"Really? It's done already?"

"Yeah. It's done."

"That's great!" A minute later, he hung up the phone.

In my own mind, it *was* done. I had already set aside the time; cleared it with my wife; knew it was coming up. Gary wouldn't have to worry about it. But truthfully, it wasn't done.

I was tapping away on my computer late that night when I heard a key in the office door, and in walked Gary. He rarely comes into the office late at night, particularly after an exhausting road trip. But there he was, just as surprised to see me as I was to see him.

"John! What are you doing here?"

"Well, I'm finishing up the magazine article."

"Oh! But I thought you said that was finished."

"Well ..."

Out of my strong desire to please and serve, I had been afraid to admit I was falling behind. Instead I lied, even if it was a "white lie" so he wouldn't worry while he was on a trip. I'm sorry to say that it resulted in a major stress in our relationship for a few days. And the very things I was trying so hard to avoid by not being totally honest—losing positional power, distressing my best friend, and telegraphing that I was having to work all night to meet my deadlines—were the very things that happened! It would have been better to admit the truth in the first place instead of trying to "manage my image."

That incident was a wake-up call to quit protecting my always-under-perfect-control mirage. I did what we'll encourage you to do in chapters 12, 13, and 14: I admitted my failure to Gary, my wife, my small group, and a close friend, and I asked for forgiveness and added strength from my heavenly Father. And at Today's Family, we did what we should have done months before: We hired an administrative assistant to help us with an overflowing workload.

Life usually works that way. When we own up to our limitations and frailties—our humanity—we find that people actually draw closer to us. While it wasn't easy, I found far more acceptance in admitting I had blown it and asking for support and accountability than I ever did trying to appear perfect. For some strange reason, most folks seem to identify with someone who doesn't know it all and can't do it all!

One of our friends, a professor at a Bible college in California, told us about a long-standing battle with lustful thoughts. It was a lonely battle,

When we own up to our limitations and frailties—our humanity—we find that people actually draw closer to us.

too. Because he's a Christian teacher, he didn't dare let anyone know he had a private world haunted by impure thoughts and mental adulteries.

Finally, however, gathering up his courage, he called a man in another ministry—a man he didn't know that well but deeply respected for his godly life-style—and invited him to lunch. As they sat in a back booth of the restaurant, our friend haltingly admitted his struggle and asked for prayer. Rather than driving the other man away in disgust as he feared might happen, his candor allowed the two to strike up a friendship that day. Since that time, they've shared many lunches and have even launched a long-term project together.

Men caught up in the mirage of image management are consumed with maintaining a cool, detached, I-don't-need-anyone exterior. Keeping a glossy shine on that public self becomes even more important than developing inner character. It means polishing the gold sword rather than picking it up. And the real men they want to be lose the battle to the cardboard men they've created.

If you, too, are tempted at times to "talk a good game," step right on in to a meeting of "Image Managers Anonymous." Pull up a chair. You'll find plenty of company inside, including a prestige-hungry newspaper publisher, a struggling college professor, and a couple of guys named Smalley and Trent who may not know much but know enough to realize they're not perfect. We also know there is help available from concerned friends, from family, and from an all-knowing-but-still-merciful God. But only if we ask ... and never if we stay hidden behind a false image of perfection.

Someone told us recently that Moses wandered in the desert for 40 years because he refused to stop and ask for directions! There's all kinds of help for image-conscious guys like us. The catch is, you have to ask.

Five roadblocks. Each with more than enough power to take the gold sword from our hands, blunt its power, cause it to rust, or keep it out of our reach. Yet as we've mentioned all along, there are solutions, answers to what holds us back so that we don't spend a lifetime wondering "what could have been."

The help we need begins as we look at perhaps the greatest source of power God has given His people ... found in the midst of a group of friends. This power is so strong that it's like a ten-strand nylon rope!

CHAPTER 12

THE HIDDEN POWER OF FRIENDS

As authors, we agonize over the thought of putting one of the most important chapters we've ever written in the last part of a book. It fits here logically, but the concept shared in these pages is vital to every man who wants to carry the gold sword, as well as to every family and every church family across our world.

In this chapter, you'll discover the most powerful way we know to infuse encouragement, motivation, and even positive correction into a person's life. It's the same key Jesus gave the apostles in constructing the early church, and we've seen it build and maintain the qualities of a great swordsman in a man's life. Equally important, it provides the greatest source of protection we know of from the incredible pressures facing the family today. You'll see this hidden power unfold through the story of Kyle and Ann.

A SECRET SOURCE OF STRENGTH

All of us face storms in life, but not everyone has a shelter from the storm. Thankfully, Kyle and Ann did. And if that shelter hadn't been there for them to run to, their marriage and family would have been shattered on the rocks.

Kyle and Ann live in a typical home in a typical suburb in southern

California. They have two children, two cars, and the typical struggles that every couple faces. But what isn't typical is something Kyle and Ann committed themselves to several years ago that saved their marriage.

For 15 years, Kyle and Ann had weathered life's storms together. At times, their problems were like gale-force winds, but their marriage had never come close to capsizing—that is, until recently.

In the midst of financial and extended family problems, Kyle finally felt he'd reached the breaking point. Tired of the storm winds and of being driven emotionally night and day, in a tirade, he decided the only option left to him was to desert his wife and family.

Kyle tried to jump ship, but tied around his life was a line of support and accountability that kept him from going under ... and his family from running aground.

Without realizing it, Kyle and Ann had made one of the most important decisions of their married life when they joined a support group of other couples. Over the months, they had strengthened their support lines to the point that when Kyle began packing, Ann went to the phone and immediately called Terry, another man in the group. Within minutes, Terry had called Mike, yet another man in their group.

Like a 9-1-1 alert, the message went out that Kyle and Ann were in trouble. And after a response time that would make any fire chief proud, Kyle was staring at his two friends.

For months, these men had met weekly, usually on Saturday morning at 6:00 A.M., sharing each other's burdens, talking about financial woes or marital frictions. On any given Saturday, they might be going through a book together, or one man might have a particular verse to share. But always there was time to pray for each other, to listen, to encourage.

And while they didn't have it written down, in unwritten words their small group provided two essential ingredients that would prove the difference between Kyle and Ann's falling apart or staying together.

First Terry drove over and talked to Kyle, offering the emotional support of a close friend. Later, Kyle said that his time with Terry was like having an ice pack and a splint applied to a wrenched ankle. Shortly after that, Mike arrived, providing another dose of encouragement and support.

Since they were both joggers, Mike suggested, "Let's talk while we're running around the block." And as Kyle let out built-up physical steam in their four trips around the block, even more importantly, he let go of the dam of emotional pressure that had built up in his life.

His time with Mike was a period of repentance, cleansing, and healing. As they walked and ran together, Kyle finally broke down and began to cry. For the first time in years, he let down all his burdens.

That's what it can mean to be part of a small group—having a friend to stand beside you; to put his arm around you when you're weeping; to provide comfort and conversation that lead you to a decision you knew all along was right; to stay with your family and work things out; and in the weeks to come, someone to walk with as you're healing.

From the time Jesus left us to live out the Christian life, He put us in groups, small centers of support—yet big enough to give us the help we desperately need during times of trouble, and major encouragement for positive growth.

While Terry and Mike supported Kyle, their wives, Gail and Shirley, were there for Ann. And the result was that instead of becoming another single-parent home in the sea of heartache, Kyle and Ann became a shelter from the storm. A place of repair. And a safe place for children to grow up without fear of sinking ships.

The two keys that held Kyle to his family were the lifelines of *support* and *accountability* within their small group. But how many other Kyles and Anns ended up jumping overboard that day, thinking it would be easier just to swim to a new start—only to be caught in riptides of emotional pain that could drag them under?

If no other message in this book hits home with you, our prayer is that this one will. For from the time Jesus left us to live out the Christian life, He put us in groups, small centers of support—yet big enough to give us the help we desperately need during times of trouble, and major encouragement for positive growth.

In case you have any doubts about the importance of a small group in helping you carry your gold sword, let's look at just eight of the many benefits you'll enjoy every day when you have that lifeline of support.

EIGHT BENEFITS YOU GAIN FROM A SUPPORT GROUP

1. INCREASED LIFE SPAN, AND DECREASED SUSCEPTIBILITY TO SICKNESS

How would you like to strengthen your immune system, making it easier for your body to fight off disease? Increase your life expectancy, in some cases by as much as two years? Even reduce your insurance bills by dramatically lowering your chances of getting in a car accident?

Now, before you think we're about to pull out our slides and explain the latest multi-level way to health, wealth, and success, let's add a few *more* positives, this time listing benefits to your emotional health.

How would you like to be listened to and not receive a lecture when you have hurts to share? To feel the deep support of people who accept you for who you are? And even to have someone with the courage to be honest about a problem area in your life, yet without condemning?

Sound like a script for a remake of "Fantasy Island"? Actually, it's happening in family rooms all across the country. And it's the very thing we're calling men everywhere to make a commitment to. *Today, specifically, we're calling you.*

There's no product you can grab off the shelf, nor is this a one-time proposition. It's a *process* men and women can choose to be part of that can pay incredibly positive benefits to their health.

A recent study was done with a group of widows whose spouses had died by either suicide or accident. One year after the death of their partners, the widows were asked to indicate how they had responded to what happened, as well as to list the health problems they had encountered during the last year. The results were striking:

•The more frequently subjects discussed their spouse's death with other people—in the supportive context of a small group—*the fewer health problems they experienced.*[1]

•The more they brooded about the death, not discussing it with others, *the more and greater health problems they had!*[2]

Or look at studies of people with cancer. Again, a definite link was

136

shown between a person's attitude and openness about sharing his problem with a supportive small group and how long he lived following surgery.[3]

Even the common cold strikes those in small groups less than it does others! Perhaps, in part, this is why people who attend church are in better health than those who do not. And they live longer as a result![4]

It's with good reason that the Scriptures command us not to forsake the gathering of ourselves together.[5] Ignore it or not, there's a deep need within each of us, male or female, to unload hurts and feelings in a healthy way, and to take to heart sound counsel. And the best place we've seen for this type of sharing is in the energizing, strengthening process of a small group.

As we saw earlier, in addition to all the physical benefits, there are powerful emotional benefits. To see how this works, consider a typical man who lives in our fast-paced world. Let's see how he handles the pressure either with or without a support group.

Jim is facing major stress in his job. Deadlines are looming, his staff has been cut back, and without a miracle, he won't finish on time the major project he's been given. That's *stress*.

At the same time, his elderly mother is experiencing major health problems. Three times today, he has had to run out to help her. *Stress*.

His work has been taking so much time, his wife feels neglected and is putting pressure on him to spend more time with her. *Stress*.

And now the baby has a cold and is waking up at all hours of the night. *Stress*.

Then there's that church leaders' meeting on the budget Thursday night that he can't miss. *Stress*.

Now his beeper's going off again! *Stress!*

Where does Jim go to deal with these pressures? For the average Jim across our country, nowhere. He just bows his back, digs down deeper ... and puts himself more at risk. Why? Because of something called *immunocompetence*.

When Jim gets under stress, his body goes on alert. That means many glands go into action, dumping a number of enzymes and chemicals into his bloodstream. Two of those chemicals are adrenaline, which gets us ready to run or fight, and endorphins, which provide a natural pain suppressor in anticipation of our getting hurt.

If we're being chased by a bear for a short time, adrenaline and endorphins are terrific chemicals to have in our systems! But Jim's stress isn't a hundred-yard dash; it has been a nine-month marathon. In fact, it has gone on nonstop all summer and fall, and now, with Christmas looming, it looks as if it will be next summer before he gets a break!

But while Jim isn't getting a break, those two chemicals constantly being pumped into his system are beginning to break down. And in the simplest of terms, one by-product of adrenaline breakdown can be chemically induced clinical depression. Too many endorphins can clog the

By holding everything inside, we actually make a choice to allow our health to deteriorate.

immune system, impairing its ability to fight off illness.[6]

How significant a problem is this? In laboratory animals, those with "immunosuppression" such as we've described were more likely to get sick, even to grow tumors. And the same thing is true with dogs' best friend—us!

By holding everything inside, Jim is actually making a choice to allow his health to deteriorate. By not opening up and sharing his hurts, struggles, fears, and burdens with someone or some group, he's repeating what has been shown in a number of studies.

But if he's wise enough to join a small group, he will have found one of the best ways to protect his health. There's amazing health in a comforting hug from a friend; hearing the joy of another couple's victory last week; having someone say, "Can we just pause and pray for you?" Jim gets those blessings along with seven other powerful benefits each time he shows up!

2. LOVING SUPPORT TO HOLD UP YOUR SWORD, BOTH LOCALLY AND NATIONALLY

I (Gary) can say from personal testimony that the biggest help in taking up and hanging on to my own gold sword has been the small groups I've been a part of for years. In fact, during the late 1970s, for a period of 3 years, Norma and I were in 3 different groups that together numbered almost 30 couples. As close friends, we would meet once a week and pray for and encourage each other. And as Kyle and Ann experienced, we met a crucial need in each others' lives: the loving support of a few good friends.

Years later, when many of us in those original groups met for a reunion, we realized that not one of the couples who regularly attended ever separated or divorced. That's not to say there weren't problems. Several couples' relationships were strained almost to the point of divorce, but the warm, loving support of the group got them through the crisis and helped rebuild loving relationships.

What do we mean specifically when we write of gaining "support"? And why is it such an important benefit today?

Actually, the support of men for other men is ages old. In the Old Testament, we see a dramatic story of how, without the support of a few friends, a great battle would have been lost.

Under the command of Joshua, the army of Israel fought bravely against the Amalekites. But victory was far from certain. Whether or not Israel would prevail depended on a miracle.

From his vantage point on top of a hill, Moses saw that as long as he held up the staff of God in his hands, Israel was winning the battle. But when he lowered his hands, the tide turned in favor of the Amalekites. So Moses bravely stood and held up the staff.

It was inevitable, however, that his strength would begin to wane ... his arm to drop slowly ... and Israel would go down to defeat. But that didn't happen. Why? One word—*support*.

Aaron stood on one side of Moses, helping him hold up one hand. And Hur stood on the other side, supporting his other hand. The result was a great victory for Israel that day.[7]

That's exactly what we're calling men to do with men today—to stand next to a brother who's committed to holding up his gold sword in the battle for his family. And should his strength ever subside, he's got someone right there to help him hold up his sword and win the victory.

With all the pressures and trials we face, it's hard to stand alone. And the fact is, we don't have to. Scripture tells us that if one can make a thousand flee, two can make ten thousand flee![8] There is power in linking up with a group that can help us be the men we're called to be.

Actually, there are two types of groups we would encourage you to link up with, one *a local support group* and the other *a national support group* for men.

With a local support group, *you gain three specific types of support each time you meet—factors we'll describe in this section.* There's also a national support group to which we want to introduce you. We're proud to be part of this men's organization called Promise Keepers.[9] Through its excellent materials, pastors' and leadership conferences, and a massive once-a-year national rally, your local support group can be linked to men all across our country who are also committed to going for the best with their God, marriage, and family.

But it all begins with your hometown group that can provide the three types of support you need to stay strong.

A. Support comes from hearing words of praise.

We encourage all small groups, including our own Homes of Honor groups, to begin each session with some type of praise or affirmation for each person, preferably coming from one's mate.

Hearing your spouse praise you week after week can be a powerful source of encouragement. I (Gary) discovered this myself when Norma would praise something I had done or some attitude I'd conveyed that week.

Like waiting to be surprised when opening a present, I actually looked forward to attending those small group meetings and having her "unwrap" her praise. And I wasn't alone. I noticed that even the most conflictful couple began to look forward to this time of praise—even if it felt mechanical initially. As John and I have led groups ever since, people have continually appreciated this simple time of affirmation.

Some men work for bosses or deal consistently with relatives who are experts at criticism. They especially need and can get from a small group the affirmation of close friends.

B. Support comes from appropriate, meaningful touch.

Placing your hand on another's shoulder while gently saying something like, "I know this relationship seems impossible to keep together at times, but we're here for you. We love you, and we know it will get better" can speak far more than the words alone. Both a physical and an emotional benefit come from appropriate touch, and this is another helpful part of a small-group experience.[10]

Obviously, there can be complications from men hugging women other than their wives in the group, and vice versa. Some people may have come from abusive backgrounds, too, where the only touching was in the context of anger; they may resist even a handshake or a pat on the back.

But all of us have our own touch bank. And appropriately touching someone who is hurting can convey a message of support and bonding that can make positive deposits into that person's account.

Biblically, there are numerous examples of Christ's touching and laying His hands on others. Other believers displayed physical touch as well. And within the bounds of all purity, we've seen women hug another woman in the group, and men put an arm around another man, and that very act of touch provided a major breakthrough in the lives of the hurting individuals.

C. Support comes through words of hope.

Simple statements like these can make a powerful difference to a struggling person: "We can do it together." "Whatever it takes, I'm here for you." "If we need to listen to you each week for a year, it's okay. You're going to get through this." "With the Lord's help, we can hold on together."

Often a couple who are discouraged with trying to improve and not seeing any results need a picture of a hopeful future. That's why it's so important to hear such words of encouragement regularly, words that can come from a small group.

And if we gain the benefit of massive support to hold up our swords in a small group, we also receive something equally powerful—an increase in desire and motivation to accomplish our personal and family goals—it's called *accountability*.

3. HIGHER MOTIVATION TO DO WHAT'S RIGHT

Have you ever suffered from a lack of motivation? Not just the desire to pull the covers back over your head when the alarm goes off on a cold winter's morning, but the lack of inner resolve to deal with a small problem before it becomes a large one. To make that father-daughter date you've talked about a reality, not just a goal. To finally confront your father in an honest, loving way—face to face, not just in your dreams. Or to follow through on so many good ideas you've heard at conferences or at church but somehow have been left in a notebook or forgotten on the walk to your car.

This other important benefit of a small group is the every-week encouragement to do your best and *be* your best. It's the accountability you get when a support person asks a simple question like "How's it going this week?" or "What happened when you did your homework?" or "What's one way you could solve that problem this week?" It's great to have a personal cheerleading squad, people who are going to appreciate your efforts and reward them with a "Well done!" People pulling for you to make it, not blow it. People who will say, "That's great!" and clap and cheer when you make progress. But a *super* motivational charge comes when loving people ask if you did last week what you promised to do.

For some men, particularly those who have suffered a difficult past, internal motivation is hard to drum up. In fact, one secular best-selling book captures this problem in its title: *Passive Men and Wild Women!* The author puts his finger on a common problem across our country—namely, a number of men tend to be more passive or slower in developing good relationships than their spouses. The loving support and *accountability* of a small group is a major part of the solution.

When a man struggles to take an active role in family decisions, to be the spiritual leader in the home, to get involved in the lives of his children, or even to work at putting bread on the table, pressure can build to the breaking point in a home. Often without realizing it, his inactivity has become a purposeful choice. If he sits still long enough (usually just as Dad did), the pressure will finally catapult his wife into a frenzy of activity, and she'll do the job he's supposed to handle.

Soon, instead of a marriage team, you've got only one player on the field, and she's exhausted from carrying the gold sword all alone! The more passive the man gets, the wilder she becomes, and the worse the model they both provide to the children, who don't miss a moment of the battle.

Men, it may be a hard pill to swallow, but laziness is a learned activity. Even for committed procrastinators, however, there is hope. Without exception, the men we've seen in counseling who struggle with a lack of motivation *are not in small groups.* But we've seen time and again that when men finally join a healthy group, things begin to change. Why? Because of that same, powerful one-two punch of loving support and healthy accountability that brings things in the darkness into the light—and works equally well on both of them.

Waiting on an unmotivated, undisciplined man to follow through is one of the most frustrating things a wife can experience. And what often happens is that even when such a man gets convicted and starts to take some small steps toward responsibility, the wife is so angry by then that she criticizes his baby steps, hindering any attempts he makes to walk!

The positive atmosphere of a small group provides the antidote to this extremely hurtful problem. The man gets the support and encouragement to take those first steps toward change, and he receives applause from the group when he takes them. The wife gets the support and accountability to hang in there with him, to talk about the frustration, and even to learn to encourage his efforts, which can then lead to greater successes.

We live in a hostile world. Most of us don't have a week go by in which we're not blasted, bounced, or criticized by someone. But what a breath of fresh air it is to know there's a rest stop in your week, surrounded by the positive elements of a small group!

These first three benefits of small-group participation are great, but they're only a start! The next is one of the most important of all.

4. GAIN SELF-CONTROL OVER UNWANTED HABITS AND THOUGHTS

There's nothing more powerful than a deep, inner sense of self-control. And it's a power you can develop in a small, supportive group of gold sword carriers.

... It's the strength to keep your tongue still at work when everyone else is ripping the boss to shreds behind his back.

... It's the resolve to turn past the "Adults Only" movie channel in the hotel room, even when you're all alone and it's late at night.

... It's the courage to count to ten ... and then to ten again ... instead of ripping into your spouse or teenagers when they irritate you.

In Proverbs, we read that *"he who is slow to anger is better than the mighty, and he who rules his spirit, than he who captures a city."*[11]

Ruling your spirit. Keeping tabs on your temper. Slowing down your reactions so you behave responsibly instead of selfishly. These are earmarks of self-control, true masculinity, and men who carry the gold sword. And they speak of something else as well.

The degree of self-control you have is in direct proportion to the degree of self-acceptance you have. Put another way, if you don't value yourself, you won't "pull in the reins" on negative actions and attitudes. In biblical Greek, one word picture behind the word *self-control* is this idea of "pulling in the reins" on a horse—or a habit.

The failure to "pull in the reins" lies at the heart of any budding or full-blown addiction. And what keeps our hands away from the reins too often is a deep inner sense of powerlessness and rejection—no matter how "together" we look on the outside.

Our friend Wade is a classic example of this all-too-common cycle. The son of a television celebrity, Wade grew up watching his father live out one image on the screen ... and a very different one at home. His dad was so strong and in control in each continuing TV episode, yet so totally controlled by the bottle when he stepped away from the cameras.

Wade grew up resenting his father and, in a deeper way, disliking him-

> *The degree of self-control you have is in direct proportion to the degree of self-acceptance you have.*

self for being like him in many ways. Wade became a master at keeping up two images. The outer image was someone under control, charming, charismatic—just like Dad. But his inner self wouldn't pull the reins in on his escalating drinking problem until it turned around and bit him.

A successful life is built from the inside out.[12] But Wade tried to reverse the process. By never filling in the hole in his heart (see chap. 10), he let a deep inner dislike for himself smolder into flames.

It wasn't until he lost his job and his family to his drinking that he finally had to confront his problems and became a committed member of a distinctively Christian Alcoholics Anonymous group. He told us, "I used to blame everything on my father. But then I saw that the enemy was actually me.

"People would praise me for something I'd accomplish, but I'd never really believe it. I had a beautiful wife, an outstanding ministry, but I hated myself. And my closet drinking was just one more way to prove to myself that I really *wasn't* valuable—no matter what anyone else said.

"For somebody who set out to 'never be like my dad,' I did a great job of becoming just like him."

Men, it's time we faced ourselves and admitted it. *We can't pull ourselves out of a hole like that by ourselves.* It takes the two things I (Gary) heard Chuck Colson tell a group of newly released prisoners they'd need to keep from ending up right back in prison: *the power of God in their lives, and a close friend.*

Whether you're hooked on cable television channels, sexual temptation, out-of-control spending, overeating, or substance abuse—whether you're caught up in the first steps of any addiction or 20 miles down the road to ruin—you've got hope! At least you do if you've got those 2 things in your life. And even better than a single close friend is a small group of close friends to give you that support and accountability.

We're all facing our own personal battles. But once we feel the incredible support of someone "holding up our arms" in a support group, something else tremendous happens. Some of us, for the first time in our lives, will actually begin to *feel* more valuable as people and as a result experience major growth. Still not convinced? Then read on and see how it happens.

5. Dramatically Increased Self-Worth

Would you like to feel as valuable inside as God intends? Would you like to have the self-confidence to be thankful for your strengths and honest about your weaknesses?

Those are just two marks of someone who has a strong sense of self-worth and of how God values him. And once again, the best environment we know of where a person's self-worth can develop is in the loving support of a small group.

The fastest-growing churches know this and are filled with small groups. The largest churches in the world know it, and they're built on small groups, too. (Remember that the early church was a house church—men and women meeting in small groups!)

What happens when someone refuses to base his sense of worth on what Jesus says about him and forsakes the strengthening agent God designed the church to be? Almost without exception, you've got someone with a hole in his heart from the past. And a person with such an inner hurt and dislike of self will always feel worthy only of failure, never success.

To bring this down to basics, let's take a look at a commonplace happening in a common work setting.

Jim is a new employee, working on the shipping docks because it's the only job available. He's hardworking, doesn't abuse coffee breaks, and seems way overqualified to turn big piles into little piles.

What's the natural thing to do with Jim after a few months of exemplary service? Promote him, of course! He's obviously capable of handling more responsibility, and even of overseeing the work of others.

What the employer misses, however, is that Jim has a "hole" in his heart. Because his view of his personal worth is distorted on the low side, it's as if he has a self-destruct switch, ready to be thrown at the first sign of success.

On a one-to-ten scale, let's say Jim's innermost sense of self-worth is about a two. That came from an abusive father, an overcontrolling mother, failed potential, and consistently ruining promising relationships with the "right" girl.

With two years of college behind him and a truckload of untapped talent, he looks like what he should become—a leader! He even realizes that working as the lowest man on the shipping dock is a "two" of a job. But the problem is, it feels so comfortable.

What happens next is what has happened before. He gets called into the boss's office and is given a major promotion. Now, instead of being in a job that's a "two," he's placed in a position of high value where he needs to be assertive and have self-control. It's an "eight" of a job, with the pay and privileges to go with it. So what happens next?

Does Jim live up to the challenge and make his mark on the company? Or does he self-destruct and reinforce his mark of lost potential as he picks up his severance check?

You make the call.

If you said he'd self-destruct, you'd be right *more than 90 percent of the time*. Why? Because a person who views himself as a "two" in either business or personal relationships will actually begin to provoke others to treat him that way! And one of the easiest ways to make sure you fail is to try to build a healthy, functional, successful life on an inner belief of low worth. This also, as we mentioned, happens at home. If our wives feel like "twos," they can be self-destructive.

What happens to Jim? He sleeps through his alarm three straight mornings and misses the supervisors' meeting three times in a week. He "forgets" to mark down a three-hour lunch break on a friend's time card, but an audit by his superior helps jog his memory. His dress becomes sloppy, his drive runs out of gas, and his productivity drops.

In only a few weeks, he has self-destructed and is out of work, looking for a place he can be comfortable, even if he's miserable. And not surprisingly, he'll usually take another "two" job, since that's how he looks at himself on the inside.

If you're tired of failure and the damage caused by feelings of low self-worth, you have some options. You can turn to chapter 13 and see how to find a skilled person to help you begin to deal with hurts from the past. And you can do what all good counselors usually recommend—take the additional step of joining a small support group.

Habits of the heart can be easily formed ... and difficult to break. But they *can* be broken. It's possible to gain the self-worth needed for successful relationships. But not without a friend and a group. And not without filling the hole in our hearts.

A longer and healthier life. Loving accountability. The motivation to do what's right with your wife and children. Control over unwanted habits. Even a boost in your self-worth to where God wants it. If we stopped here, we'd have a tremendous list of benefits! But like receiving a certified letter saying a present is coming for you, there are still three life-changing benefits waiting for you to unwrap by being in a small support group.

6. "Reparenting" for Closeness

Dr. Bill Retts,[13] a friend we've gone to for counseling and one of the most insightful therapists we know, often pictures what he does as hour-long lessons in "reparenting." As we've seen, if a boy misses out on those aspects of interaction with a parent that build closeness, it can leave a hole in his heart as an adult and an often-unhealthy desire for distance in relationships. But just like bad habits and low self-worth, an exaggerated distance is hard to maintain when you're in the middle of a small group that's committed to being close.

Like it or not, the group leader is often looked up to in a parental role, and that's not all bad. Some of us had such poor models in our fathers or mothers (or both) that we've been left to piece together a puzzle without getting to see the picture on the box!

We met recently with a leading authority on church growth through small groups. He said that a major factor in the great success of such groups is the opportunity they provide for reparenting. In a small group, he said, hurting individuals often receive the parental blessing withheld from them as kids.

If we've missed out on the positive interaction of a father and mother in our growing-up years, the opportunity to experience it through the leader

147

and other couples in the group is tremendous. For some people, it's their first close-up view of what healthy interaction can be. While we'll never be young again, we can be "reparented" in the right direction by a loving

> *If we've missed out on the positive interaction of a father and mother in our growing-up years, the opportunity to experience it through the leader and other couples in the group is tremendous.*

heavenly Father through one of His best means of encouragement, a small group.

At the same time, others who have grown too close for comfort—and emotional health—can also benefit from joining a group.

7. HEALTHY INDEPENDENCE

There's a verse of Scripture used in almost all wedding ceremonies that usually gets as much attention as a distant relative standing in the reception line. Yet within that one sentence is a key to successful relationships—and another important reason each of us needs the strength offered in a small group.

The verse? "For this reason a man shall *leave* his father and mother and *cleave* to his wife."[14]

Notice the stair-step progression that must take place for a marriage to become complete. First comes leaving; then comes cleaving. First comes independence from the past; then there can be a healthy interdependence in the present.

But many men who grew up in a feminized environment skip over independence and opt for overdependence. They settle for becoming "people pleasers" rather than gaining a healthy sense of personal responsibility. The popular word for "people pleasers" today is the catchword *codependent*.

Who are these people? They're the ones who, when they're drowning, have everybody *else's* life flash in front of their eyes!

Seriously, they're well-meaning people who push their nurturing skills far out of balance. They are incredibly good at anticipating and meeting the needs of others, but they fail to come up with a direction or dream for themselves.

While this used to be a particularly feminine ailment, the ranks of codependent men are growing rapidly. And like their female counterparts, they become so unhealthily connected with others that they can't step beyond someone else's agenda to make up their own—or to say the simple word *no*.

Russ was a textbook example of this type of man. The youngest of three boys, with the other two being deaf, he became the only connecting link between the mounting problems of the children and his parents' crumbling marriage.

Russ's father and mother wouldn't speak to each other directly. So for years they spoke through him.

"Go tell your mother I'm not going to eat that slop she fixed for dinner tonight."

"Oh, yeah? Go back and tell your father he's a *#+*##!!!!"

And as the only one in the family who could use sign language, he was also the interpreter for every conversation between his parents and two angry, rebellious brothers.

At seven and eight years of age, he had to stop fistfights as well as put out verbal fires of scorn, hostility, and contempt that would have challenged an experienced clinical psychologist. And while he became an expert "people pleaser" in trying to keep his family together, he paid a terrible price.

Russ became so supersensitive to pleasing everyone around him and thus avoiding pain that it left no place for healthy personal growth. And it set him up to get ulcers.

When Russ grew up and entered the work force, he was an exceptional employee. Just pile more and more on his desk, and "good old Russ" would get it done (even if it meant coming in many nights and most weekends). He made his boss look great ... but he never once asked for or was given a significant raise or promotion.

Of course, his heightened sensitivity also made him a real catch for his wife. ("At last I've found a sensitive man!") But what she landed was a passive-aggressive man with a terrible problem, an inability to say no. She thought he would take the role of headship in the family, but he looked to her to do it—resentfully. Russ had been trained to submit with the best of them, but so much so, and so out of balance, that it left his wife no way to exercise *her* God-given function.

Because Russ had grown up with almost no space between family members, if one person signaled a left turn, they all headed that way. When you're a committed people pleaser, afraid of losing relationships, the only direction you can turn is where everyone else wants to go. And soon that was true in his marriage as well.

If one night he really wanted spaghetti—they'd go eat fish again if that's what she wanted. For almost a year, he was convinced they needed a four-wheel-drive vehicle. He bought all the auto magazines, even checked the paper each day for one they could get at a steal. But the weekend she said they had to get the new vehicle, he settled for the station wagon she wanted—and another handful of Tums.

> *In a small group of committed friends, you can be held accountable for taking steps toward healthy independence.*

To say no to someone significant in his life was somehow unloving, unkind, and un-American! But his inability to say it was really unhealthy. And if you struggle with saying no to your spouse or others, the same is true in your life.

If you're up at all hours accomplishing other people's projects because you can't say no, you're caught on the *hook* of codependency. If you don't have the emotional breathing room to express your negative feelings directly to another person, you've swallowed the *line* that "honesty is too fearful to handle." And if you don't get help in learning how to become more healthily independent, you'll swallow the *sinker* ... and end up at the bottom in all your relationships.

But didn't Jesus help and heal everyone, trying always to please them? Not the Jesus in the Bible. He knew enough not to entrust Himself to the changing opinions of men who would crown Him one day and kill Him the next. He was closely bonded to His disciples, but he remained independent enough to rebuke them for suggesting He forsake the cross. Even His daily dependence on the Father and the Holy Spirit wasn't an unhealthy co-dependence that blurred who He was, but a strengthening interdependence of the members of the Trinity.

We've already talked about people who grow up with too much distance and how their exaggerated sense of personal space can ruin their relationships. Now we've seen how too much closeness can be just as deadly. But thankfully, in the middle of two extremes is a place where we can find the balance we need.

Can you make decisions without looking over your shoulder at Mom and Dad (not for counsel, but for *permission*)? Are you able to say "I don't like that" to someone's face without unreasonable fear that the person will say "I don't like you"? And even if something you believe in isn't popular, do you have the inner strength to stand apart from the crowd and lean only on the rightness of your action?

In a small group of committed friends, you can be held accountable for taking steps toward healthy independence. As you admit this problem out loud to such a group, you'll enjoy a feeling of relief and a sense that finally, someone will help "hold up your arm" in this area. Someone will cheer on your triumphs and encourage you in your failures. And as you do begin to change, even if you meet criticism when you start to turn things around, a small group can provide both you and your spouse with the strength and encouragement to "leave" and "cleave"—and finally have the level of intimacy you've always wanted.

We've now seen seven reasons for choosing to be in a small group, each one by itself worth taking the step. But together, they're like a seven-course, nutritious meal that brings strength and energy to your life. And who's going to skip dessert, especially when it's a benefit as good as the best chocolate-and-caramel-fudge dessert ever made!

8. THE RESOURCES, REASSURANCE, AND PERSPECTIVE OF OTHERS

As a father, Mark had tried patience, subtle pressure, even occasional explosions. But nothing worked with his 20-year-old son who was still living at home without paying any rent; still unemployed after all the lectures; still surly and terribly disrespectful with his comments and demands on his mother. The young man made family life a living nightmare.

151

The only thing that kept Mark sane was prayer, and it was in a prayer time in his newly formed small group that he first unloaded his burden. As soon as he opened the door to his problem, in stepped Ron.

Ron was also new to the group. He had just turned 60 and had a full head of gray hair, all earned honestly in the process of raising 6 children. To Mark's surprise, Ron had gone through the same battle with his middle boy and had much to share with him, as did the rest of the group.

After that first meeting when Mark revealed his pain, Ron set up several lunches with him to map out a strategy Mark and his wife could follow. And finally, they pounded out a clear plan of action they knew they had to try. Convinced that it was right and that what he had done so far hadn't worked, Mark put it into motion.

The plan began with Mark's getting his son to agree, reluctantly, that he should begin paying his fair share of the rent or else move out. That meant his son had to get a job—at minimum wage if need be—to pay the modest rent he was being charged. Further, his abusive language would no longer be tolerated in the house. The penalty was losing the privilege of driving their second car.

As you can imagine, their son couldn't wait to test them. His language was particularly foul that night. Mark took the car keys—and nearly had a fight with his son, who couldn't believe his father would do something like that. For the next two weeks, life in their home was like an explosion in a fireworks factory. Mark's son bucked at the restraints placed on him like a wild stallion the first time a saddle hits his back.

Always before, Mark had crumbled at this point. His wife would also weaken seeing the two of them at each other's throats, and Mark would second-guess his commitment to being firm. But something was different this time. Much different!

They both had the active support of a couples' small group, and then there was Mark's men's group that he looked to for strength. And while he certainly didn't have to, Ron also called every day to say, "Hang in there, buddy. I'm praying for you. Don't give up! I've been there and I know it's tough, but you'll make it, and so will your son some day."

Yes, Mark was a different person. Stronger. More self-confident. Less reactive, and more in control of his emotions. He was loved up and prayed for so much by his two groups that when a month had gone by and there was no payment from his son, he calmly but firmly helped his son load his belongings in a friend's truck and moved him out of the house.

Things went from bad to worse when they found out their son had moved into an apartment with a local hellion, but Mark and his wife held their ground. Backed by the prayers and power they found in their groups, they actually grew stronger as people—and as a couple.

At last the battle was won, but not until 18 long months had passed. The day finally arrived when their son grew tired of ruining his life and decided to get a new one. Like the prodigal son returning home, he was met with tears and open arms when he showed up at the back door around supper time one evening. And two support groups cried and celebrated with the family as another lost sheep found his way home.

Today, their son could be a poster child for a tough-love group. He's in charge of the hardware aisle in a major home remodeling store by day, and he's carrying nine hours at community college at night. And thrown in for extra measure, miracle of miracles, he's even back in church.

Mark and his wife got more than they ever bargained for in their small group.

The physical benefits of reduced stress and better health during the most difficult time in their lives.

The praise, words of hope, and meaningful touches they needed so much on a consistent basis.

The loving accountability of an almost daily call from Ron and in the weekly meetings with their groups.

The motivation to do what was right—not easy—with their son.

The self-control to talk in a respectful voice while their son was screaming in disrespect.

The constant reminder from the group leader that their self-worth was based on how highly God viewed them, not on how little their son did.

The lessons in reparenting from the older group members who had been there before.

The encouragement to not become enmeshed in their adult son's problem, but to help themselves and him to come to a place of healthy independence.

And always, at each couples' or men's group meeting, they seemed to receive just the right verse, suggestion, study topic, or hug that provided the *reassurance, resources,* and *perspective* they needed so much.

Eight benefits. All eight were right at their fingertips—and are right at yours, as well, to help you be all you've wished you could be.

"But, Gary, John, you just don't understand!" you might be saying.

"We've got major problems. If we joined a group like that, *we'd ruin it!*"

You're not alone in feeling that way. Many of us feel like Groucho Marx when he said, "I wouldn't join a club that would have me as a member!"

If you're in crisis right now, go back to what never changes—the Scriptures. Read again that "only the wise seek counsel."[15] That means the

Many of us feel like Groucho Marx when he said, "I wouldn't join a club that would have me as a member!"

first step on your way to a supportive small group may be getting the help of an even smaller group.

Start with the smallest accountability group we know of ... a group made up of you, your spouse, and a godly counselor. In most cases, this relationship becomes a stepping-stone to a larger one with a small group.

When do you need to go to a counselor? We once heard a comedian say, "You know you need a counselor when you have to speak so loud in every conversation that your spouse's hair parts when you talk to her."

You know you need a counselor when you're wearing your dinner plate, not eating off it.

You know you need a counselor when there's no regular "touchie-the-toes" or you get a bop in the nose.

Seriously, *there are actually three ways to tell if you need a counselor*, and several specific requirements you need to look for in the person you choose. There are also many benefits that can be yours. These are all vitally important things in forging or maintaining your gold sword, as we'll see in the next chapter.

But first, are you ready to make the decision to join a support group? As men, we've been standing on the sidelines way too long. Our families and our country need us to join together, to pick up our swords and get back in the battle. It's time we got back on the team.

If you've heard the clear call in this book to use your power, both positionally and personally, for good ... *if you truly see your own hidden value* ... we urge you to take up the challenge as we have. Pray about it, and then pick up the challenge as your own.

After years of working on it, we've put together a program called "Homes of Honor." In it are all ten of the biblical principles we teach that form the basis of healthy relationships. We urge you to first get a copy of this program or some other plan you choose, and gather at least four other men or couples to join you. Then, once a week for the next year, provide each other the loving support and honest accountability that can help you get or keep your power in balance.

Our second challenge is to come and join us in Colorado the last weekend in July every year. There, along with what we pray will be more than 50,000 other men, we're going to jam one of the Denver-area stadiums to stand up and say:

"Yes, we know we're valuable and powerful in the lives of our families and nation. And yes, we're going to use that power to honor God, to carry our gold sword with honor, and to love our families better than we ever have before."

Every year, Lord willing, we'll be in Colorado to join you. And if you can't get to Colorado (or the stadium is sold out), why not start your own version of Promise Keepers in your city or state?

Let's get serious about what we can do to change things for good in the nineties. And that change begins with us as we ...

- Recognize how valuable and powerful we are as men
- See the twin swords we carry
- Establish a clear and agreed-upon marriage and parenting plan
- Gain the benefits of a local and national support team
- Be honest and open about pursuing counseling if we need it
- Face the roadblocks that may be hindering us
- And especially, pattern our lives after the Master of the gold sword, Jesus Christ (see chap. 14).

And then one more thing....

Meet us in Colorado
the last weekend in July, where
we can shake hands and join forces to tell
the world that men are powerful... and that
their power can be used for good!

CHAPTER 13

WHAT TO DO
WHEN NOTHING
ELSE WORKS

My (Gary's) son Greg picked up the phone one day this year and made a call that literally changed his life and redirected his goals and career plans for the future. For two years, he had a negative habit that seemed to control him. While others couldn't see it from the outside, he told me, "Dad, it was as if I'd fallen through the ice, and the water was so cold, I couldn't do anything to get out!" That is, until he picked up the phone.

This year, Norma and I picked up the phone and made a call that led to some of the most helpful insights and suggestions we've ever received. Something we had dreaded for years was finally happening. We remembered talking with our friend Dr. James Dobson about how tough it had been for him and Shirley to have their children "leave the nest." And suddenly, all three of our children were leaving at once! The adjustments from being a close family to being a close family at a distance were tough. But they were made ten times easier when we picked up the phone.

And I (John) have needed to pick up the phone this year as well. In many ways, this has been the most difficult year of my life. Cindy and I lost a baby in the fifth month of her pregnancy. My mother moved into town and then broke her back in an accident. My father was diagnosed as having cancer in his lung, and it spread quickly to his brain. As I write, he holds on to life by a thread. And on top of all that, the pressure drove to the surface several personal weaknesses that began to affect my writing and my work. Added together, there were days when I felt I was going under. But thankfully, I was able to make a call.

What we had within our reach—what you have available to you—was the ability to make a call, and by that action alone to see things begin to change for the better. What do we mean?

In the Scriptures we're told, "Only the wise seek counsel."[1] And the truth and power of those words is displayed in the fact that when people pick up the phone and call a counselor, just getting on the waiting list causes immediate improvement for them and their relationships![2]

When we recommend that people seek out a counselor, we're really telling them to seek out a coach, not a couch.

Are we saying that we and our wives actually went to counseling? And we're writing books and doing seminars? That's exactly right. We want to be wise men and women. And in the times when we sat and talked with our friends, Dr. Bill Retts and Dr. Greg Crow, we gained insight, perspective, and helpful coaching on areas we could grow in immediately. In fact, we're really not aware of anyone who couldn't benefit from one or more sessions with a personal relationship "research adviser."

It used to be that the mention of going to a counselor conjured pictures of laying on a couch for hundreds of hours—at more than $100 an hour. But that's not true today. In fact, when we recommend that people seek out a counselor, we're really telling them to seek out a coach, not a couch—someone who can, in most cases, spend 6 to 12 sessions diagnosing, listening, reflecting, encouraging, and helping to build skills into our lives that can make a significant difference.

How do we know when we need a counselor?

First, those who come from dysfunctional homes will benefit from the counsel of a good book and perhaps a "talking book"—a trained therapist. What constitutes a dysfunctional home? Aren't *all* homes dysfunctional to some degree?

To some extent, yes. But there are three things to look for on a moderate-to-severe scale. Just rate your family background for these three things on a 1 to 10 scale (1 meaning "never present," and 10 meaning "always present").

1. Physical and/or emotional abuse ____
2. Obvious or persistent subtle neglect ____
3. A home where discipline was replaced by indulgence ____

If your home rates a seven or higher in any or all of these categories, then to be perfectly honest, you're a candidate for sound counsel. For many, that counsel can come through a book that deals with our past (e.g., *The Blessing*[3] or an excellent newer resource called *When Victims Marry*[4]). But if the trauma was deep and the pain flows deep, it may be time to see a counselor.

Second, if you grew up in a home that tied you up in "double binds," you may well need help. What's a double bind?

The classic picture of this type of home usually includes a mother who holds out her arms and says, "Come here and give me a hug." But when a child does go over and hug her, she's stiff and distant.

The child steps back, confused at the response, and she says, "What's the matter? Don't you love me?" or "Don't touch me. You don't really love me!"

From a distance, we can see the double message here. But in the close confines of a family, it's not so easy to pick out. And unfortunately, it's the same message many fathers give that can be extremely destructive. Take Larry's father, for example.

Larry's father gave him two powerful messages. The man was home every night, always in the overstuffed chair in front of the fireplace and television in the basement, and always unavailable to talk to Larry. What was the double message there?

"I'm always here ... but you can never come to me."

Hurts, needs, fears, joy. It didn't matter. His father was always around, but never in reach. And that's just one message. How about Steve's dad?

His father was extremely critical of him every time he did anything. "If you were worth anything as a man," Steve's father would say as he awakened him on a typical Saturday, "you'd get your lazy head up and help me clean the garage. You're under orders from a working man now!"

But Steve could never do anything good enough or fast enough to please his father. The double message in this home was "If you're a man, you need to be working." However, "You can't do any of this work right, so you must not be a man."

Today, Steve doesn't look at himself as a man. He's a recovering homosexual who rejected masculinity when he rejected his father and the destructive double-bind message his dad gave him.

Experimentally, you can drive dogs crazy by placing them in a double-bind situation. For example, an animal has two colored shapes shot onto a screen in front of him by a slide projector—perhaps a circle and an egg-shaped oval.

Both shapes begin to spin in place, the circle turning smoothly, the egg tumbling irregularly. The dog is then taught to "choose" either the circle or the egg to get a reward. That's when the real experiment begins.

Now, every time the circle changes color (by means of a different slide), the dog gets a shock. And the only way to avoid the shock is to choose the egg shape. But through the experimenter's manipulation, the oval becomes more and more round! The dog will grow increasingly anxious, as his only hope for escape—the egg shape—becomes more like the circle that issues the shock. And as the two shapes become increasingly one and the two "choices" look like pain and pain, the dog will "experimentally" go crazy.

Sound like abuse? So, too, is the emotional torment that many boys and girls go through when they're forced by a mom or dad to choose between the two shocking choices of a double bind.

"I need to be married or something is wrong with me ... but no girl I'm going to meet is ever going to be good enough."

"I need to be independent for my sake ... but every message I receive as an only child begs me to stay a child for my parents' sake."

If you come from a family where you've been driven somewhat "crazy" by the double, unfulfillable messages of a dysfunctional home, get help. It's difficult to set up a reality-based home of your own if you've never experienced it. And with the aid of a trained counselor, you can begin to see the embedded messages in your background and get them out in the light of God's presence to work on.

WHAT TO LOOK FOR IN A COUNSELOR

We know it's difficult to find a skilled counselor. But we also know there are more resources and genuinely helpful people in the field today than ever before. And more are coming from a number of fine schools across the country.

The best counselors today use short-term, action-oriented therapies that really provide help. And to further assist you in selecting a therapist, we next offer five reasons to avoid a particular counselor.

1. The dust on his⁵ Bible is more than three inches thick.

It's important that the counselor you go to be a committed Christian. That doesn't mean every session becomes a Bible study or prayer meeting, but it also doesn't mean that those important activities are totally ignored. There needs to be an understanding that what you're facing is a spiritual as well as emotional struggle.

For years, there has been a strong, anti-Christian bias in many mental health settings. We're thankful that today, there are ministries like Rapha Counseling⁶ and others across the country that have sensed this unhealthy imbalance and have moved to make sure Christian views are accepted and encouraged in the counseling process.

2. His pastor is "Rev. Sheets," and he attends the "Sanctuary of the Inner Springs" church.

Right in line with a counselor's personal commitment to Christ should be an active commitment to a local church. If you hear him saying "I don't believe in the local church," "The small groups I lead are my church," or similar statements, watch out.

We recommend getting the name of his pastor before you start counseling, and then calling and asking what he thinks of the person you've chosen. We've found that godly pastors are so sensitive about referrals that if they give a person high marks, you've gone a long way toward finding someone really helpful.

3. His own family is a wreck.

No one is perfect. Even Billy and Ruth Graham have had struggles with their children, as they've honestly and inspiringly admitted.⁷ And yes, we do believe that we're responsible for our own actions, not those of our adult children. However, you can still learn much about a person by asking about his family life.

This doesn't mean you set up a Clarence Thomas-type hearing to probe every problem the counselor had in the past. After all, many people come into the counseling profession because they have worked through problems themselves.

Having had struggles doesn't eliminate someone from being able to help ... but it also doesn't qualify the person to help. Without exception, the best counselors we've seen are those who are willing to talk about their failures as well as hang signs of success on the wall.

If the counselor you've chosen becomes extremely defensive and won't tell you a little about his background, you're probably in the wrong place.

Godly pastors are so sensitive about referrals that if they give a person high marks, you've gone a long way toward finding someone really helpful.

4. His counseling orientation is questionable.

To determine his orientation, you don't have to be an expert on all the different schools of counseling. Simply ask how he sees problems and what his approach is in dealing with them.

For example, some counselors stay fixed on past issues, never offering recommendations for what you're to do with present struggles. Others may ignore your past and look only to setting up a plan for the future. Still others may see everything as a spiritual issue, while others proclaim your problem purely emotional.

Our counsel is to look for the balance that the best counselors seem to share. This involves an understanding of how the past affects us and a willingness and commitment to help you sort through present options. In addition, there's the realization that our ultimate goal is to please and serve God and that, to a great extent, we're in a spiritual battle.

In summary, then, look for balance, and be careful of extremes.

5. Obvious sin is recommended as part of the "therapeutic" process.

Consider the "Christian" counselor who worked with a couple having sexual problems. His solution for the man? Subscribe to erotic magazines, even lay a centerfold on the pillow next to him when he and his wife were making love, as a way of exciting his passions.

Then there was the counselor who encouraged a woman to write all the poison she could in a letter to Mom and wait to read it to her until everyone was gathered around the Thanksgiving table.

Beware the counselor who tells you, "I'm an expert at 'uncoupling therapy' as well as at helping you stay together," and then suggests, after two sessions, that your "incompatibility" is grounds for divorce—and he just happens to have the name of a good divorce attorney.

We agree with our good friends Chuck and Barb Snyder, who assert that the natural "incompatibility" that comes from a man marrying a woman is not grounds enough for divorce![8] The fact that you're coming from two different directions does not have to lead to separation. We have repeatedly seen couples who were totally frozen at the North and South Poles of life move to the equator and experience all the warmth and love they longed for.

If those are some things *not* to look for in a counselor, what *should* draw you to one?

CHOOSING THE RIGHT COUNSELOR

Here are seven guidelines for choosing a good counselor:

1. The person is recommended by a godly pastor, a ministry you respect (like Focus on the Family), or friends who have already been helped by the counselor.

2. Look for someone who has the highest respect for the Scriptures.

3. Check his credentials. They do matter. The person doesn't necessarily need to have a Ph.D., but he does need solid training. There are a number of excellent counseling centers across the country: university programs like the Rosemead Graduate School of Psychology and Denver Seminary's strong counseling program (with men like Dr. Gary Oliver), and other training organizations like Dr. Larry Crabb's. Larry Crabb is a noted Christian counselor who offers extensive counselor training across the country. Our experience and feedback have been that people trained by Larry and his ministry partners, Dr. Dan Allender and Dr. Tom Varney, are often of more practical help than counselors from out-of-touch but prestigious secular institutions.

4. Do you sense a natural empathy on the counselor's part, linked with the strength to confront? In 1 Thessalonians, we see four words that are key to the counseling process. We're told to "admonish the unruly, encourage the fainthearted, help the weak, be patient with all men."[9]

Does that reflect what you feel with your counselor?

163

Some counselors are great at "admonishing" those who come into their offices. They can blast away at you each session. But can they build into your life with deep empathy and understanding as well?

Encouragement, providing help when you're weak, and long-suffering patience should be hallmarks of a Christian counselor. There is no spiritual gift of rebuke. With a good therapist, you'll find both strength and sensitivity.

5. Does the counselor treat your appointments with as much importance as he expects you to treat his advice?

If you're in week three with your counselor and the meeting time has been changed four times already, look out. Your time is valuable, as is the counselor's. If you don't see a consistency in your dealings with him (he asks you to do a homework assignment and then "forgets" to ask about it;

Encouragement, providing help when you're weak, and long-suffering patience should be hallmarks of a Christian counselor. There is no spiritual gift of rebuke.

looks at his watch more than at you; takes business calls during your session that are really not important; etc.), you may need to see someone else. Remember, he works for you!

In large part because of our writing and speaking schedule, the two of us have been forced to stop week-to-week counseling. That's also why we discourage people from flying in for "one session" in the hope that it will solve all their problems. As stated earlier, we've always found the scripture to be true that says, "Better a neighbor nearby than a brother far away."[10]

As authors, we would like to be part of that "brother far away" providing written encouragement through our books. But we would only be dishonoring people if we tried to be something we can't to those out of state. They need a "neighbor" close at hand who can help consistently.

6. He's committed to you for the long haul. Counseling is difficult. It's often draining on you, and believe us, the counselor pays a price as well. There will be times when you may not like each other for a session, or you may feel you're not getting any better. Not unexpectedly, when you first

confront problems that have been hurtful yet habitual for years, things may get worse before they improve.

What helps in the process of counseling is to look at the person's commitment to your best. If he's committed to you, cares about your struggles, and is called to his profession, you'll sense it. You'll see it in the way he prays for you outside the session. In his willingness to not let slide a problem you've been trying to ignore. In his ability to help you feel the frustration of unhealthy acts—before you do them—and then use those feelings to change.

There is great power in being loved, and you ought to feel Christ's love in the counseling office. It's a love that is both hard and soft, with the strength of a lion and the sensitivity of a lamb.[11]

7. He sees the importance of small groups and encourages you to participate—not because we think they're so important, but because, as the Scriptures say, "Two are better than one, and a strand of three, it shall be unbroken."[12]

If we're to be men of honor, men who handle well the twin swords of personal and positional power, we've got to face the facts. We need to open up and share what's on our hearts. To do so only makes us like David, a man after God's own heart. And we need to carefully consider joining a small group, and even seeing a counselor if need be.

We continually find that men are motivated to action by the deeds of other men. Actually, they always have been. And if there was ever someone who could inspire us to be our best, to pick up our gold sword, it would be the Master of the gold sword Himself. In the next chapter, you'll read how He can motivate us to become the men we were designed to be.

CHAPTER 14

MASTER OF THE GOLD SWORD

Every fall and winter weekend, men crowd around television sets to cheer on their favorite football teams. When halftime comes, they sprint to the front yard for a quick game of touch football, a game complete with spiked balls, stretched-out catches—and, we hope, no pulled hamstrings. Then everyone piles back into the house for another Diet Coke and time of cheering and yelling.

With two boys at home, I (Gary) don't think I've ever watched an entire game with my sons without somebody getting up, grabbing a ball (or a close enough facsimile, like a pillow or one of Norma's country antiques!), and starting our own all-pro game of catch in the family room.

We want this part of the book to be "halftime" for you. For 13 chapters, we've talked of our value and power as men; of discovering the gold sword; of being challenged to use it with our families and in small groups; and of overcoming roadblocks that might stand in our way.

Like the sword in the stone, the gleaming, gold handle of personal power is visible. And we've heard the promise that if we'll just walk up and grab it by the handle, it will come out of the stone, into our hands, and help us win the battle for our families.

So why do we still hesitate to pick it up? What will motivate us to move from thought or good intention to action?

Perhaps, as the apostle Paul lamented, "I do not understand what I do. For what I want to do I do not do, but what I hate to do.... For I have the desire to do what is good, but I cannot carry it out."[1]

Put another way, I can see the gold sword, and I know I need to pick it up, but I still haven't done it.

Is there an answer to this inner battle of good intentions and missed opportunities? There is if you're like the apostle who penned those lines and who had an intimate, personal relationship with the One who is truly the Master of the gold sword—the One he saw and listened to and who could provide enough motivation for a lifetime.

MASTER OF BOTH SWORDS

The Master Swordsman was born in a place called Bethlehem and grew up in a small town called Nazareth. His name was Jesus, and He carried two swords. But the sword He used most often was the one everyone least expected.

The religious leaders of Jesus' day were looking for the Messiah to come with His silver sword alone, to bring back the awesome power that caused the other nations to tremble during Moses' and Solomon's days. Jesus could have picked up that sword. When John the Baptist announced Christ, he spoke of one with incredible power: "After me will come one who is more powerful than I.... His winnowing fork is in his hand, and he will clear his threshing floor, gathering his wheat into the barn and burning up the chaff with unquenchable fire."[2]

The disciples who followed Him expected a Messiah with a silver-handled sword, a king who would shatter the iron yoke of Rome and carve out an independent Jewish state. "Lord, are you at this time going to restore the kingdom to Israel?"[3]

The great throngs who heard His teaching and saw His miracles expected a Messiah with a silver-handled sword who would reign in Jerusalem, put the Gentiles in their place, and put bread on their tables. "They began to say, 'This is the Prophet who is to come into the world.'"[4] They intended to come and make Him king by force.

Even Satan expected a Messiah with a silver-handled sword who might be dazzled by promises of power, authority, and prestige. "The devil led Him up to a high place and showed Him in an instant all the kingdoms of the world. And he said to Him, 'I will give you all their power and splendor, for it has been given to me, and I can give it to anyone I want to. So if you worship me, it will all be yours.'"[5]

No one in God's universe had a more powerful silver sword than Jesus, the Christ. No one in time or eternity had more right to bear it. And He will on the Judgment Day.

But when Christ first came to earth, He had already made the decision to lay the silver-handled sword aside for a time, along with His crown, His royal robes, and the unspeakable splendor of His majesty.

When Christ first came to earth, He had already made the decision to lay the silver-handled sword aside for a time, along with His crown, His royal robes, and the unspeakable splendor of His majesty.

After all, there wasn't much room for a silver-handled sword in the womb of His teenaged mom; in the straw-filled manger where they laid Him that Christmas night; in the little house where He toddled after Mary and played with a toy hammer; or in the carpenter shop where He helped His earthly dad.

Of course, once He passed the age of 30, there were times when He reached for His silver sword and rattled it. Like the time He instantly calmed a raging sea ... walked unharmed through an angry lynch mob ... nearly blinded the disciples with His heavenly splendor on the Mount of Transfiguration ... or commanded a stone to be rolled away from in front of the grave of a man who had been dead 4 days.

When they came to arrest Him, Peter made a halfhearted swing with a borrowed silver sword, and Jesus waved him off. "Do you think I cannot call on my Father, and He will at once put at my disposal more than twelve legions of angels?"[6] Can you imagine facing that group of silver-swordsmen?

The combined nuclear arsenals of the future world, all exploding in a millisecond, would have been a flickering firefly alongside the awesome power of the Man they came to arrest in Gethsemane. A simple word would have launched the destructive might of heaven that leveled Sodom and Gomorrah more quickly and violently than were Nagasaki and Hiroshima.

Even when they tracked Jesus down in a grove on the Mount of Olives, thinking He was just an unemployed carpenter ... a self-appointed rabbi with delusions of deity ... a Galilean rabble-rouser, leading a wild-eyed band of zealots ... they saw a glimpse of His silver sword.

"Jesus, knowing all that was going to happen to him, went out and asked them, 'Who is it you want?'

"'Jesus of Nazareth,' they replied.

"'I am he,' Jesus said....

"When Jesus said, 'I am he,' *they drew back and fell to the ground.*

"Again he asked them, 'Who is it you want?'

"And they said, 'Jesus of Nazareth.'

"'I told you that I am he,' Jesus answered."[7]

What happened to that mob of vigilantes when Jesus said, "I am..."? (He was quoting the all-powerful name that was given Moses when he asked, "'Who shall I say sent me?'... And the Lord said, 'Tell him [Pharaoh], "I am"... sent you.'"[8])

When the apostle John wrote that they "fell to the ground," he employed the same Greek term used to describe a wrestling match in the Olympics. A literal translation might read that they were pinned to the ground!

Jesus body-slammed that entire, illegally called posse with two words. Just in His voice, they caught a glimpse of His silver sword, and it pinned that hardened group of soldiers face down in the dust. *No one took Christ's life from Him. Only after He released them were they able to lay hands on Him.*

Yes, Jesus showed He had a silver sword, and He promises that He will return in judgment with it.[9] But until He comes again, He calls us to walk the way He walked. To follow His lead. To key off His example. To place the tremendous power He has given us as men under His control. *To use the gold sword.*

What does that mean?

To humble ourselves as He humbled Himself. Whenever we're with any group of people, we decide like Christ to seek their best, not our glory; with the heart of a servant, to place their needs ahead of our own. In other words...

To put our arms around children and give them priority, even when we're criticized for it, as He was.

To elevate the role of womanhood and honor and respect women, as He consistently did.

To throw a towel over our shoulders and serve frequently ungrateful, unresponsive men and women with a full heart, as He did.

To use our speech to build others up, instruct, bless, counsel, affirm, and strip away hypocrisy, as He did.

To lend the strength of our manhood and the courage of our hearts to

Jesus would say to us, "Take a different path. A narrow path. Surprise them all."

the weak, vulnerable, beaten-down, and discouraged, as He did.

To use the full measure of our personal power to gladden, lift up, heal, strengthen, renew, and chase back the darkness, as He did.

This is not what the world expects of men. Children all over the world are wounded by the careless, out-of-balance use of the silver-handled sword. Women all over the world are hurt and defensive and struggling with all their strength to blunt the reckless use of the silver-handled sword. Satan himself, who knows men's lusts and desires, encourages men to pursue the silver-handled sword alone, with all the energy of our short life span.

But Jesus would say to us, "Take a different path. A narrow path. Surprise them all. Take My gold-handled sword, and turn your world upside down."

The challenge is clearly there for us from a Master Swordsman worthy of following for a lifetime—an eternity. But how do we find the inner strength to use our gold sword each day for our families' best? He has supplied that to us as well.

RECEIVING GOD'S POWER TO USE THE GOLD SWORD

It's late at night, and you're watching an old Errol Flynn swashbuckler. He has just used his silver sword to save his king and country while dispatching dozens of the enemy! What happens in the closing scene?

He's knighted, of course. With a courtyard full of witnesses, this warrior who hasn't given an inch to the enemy freely surrenders his silver sword to one he views with higher honor.

He bows on one knee, and the king lifts the royal sword and gently taps him on each shoulder. And after that act of humility, of bowing before his king, he stands up straighter, stronger, and more respected by others than he's ever been before. A new man. A new title. And a seat reserved at the king's table and in history.

While it may seem that such heroism only works in the movies, it's really not much different from the very thing every man must do who wants to carry the gold sword. For if we're to gain God's power—have Him tap on our shoulders, so to speak—we must do three things.

1. We must acknowledge God's greatness.

When a would-be knight kneels before his king, he's recognizing that there's a power greater than his. A final place of authority. A throne to serve ... to protect ... to die for if necessary. A person he'll follow all his life who is worthy of honor.

As Christians, what kind of King do we bow before?

The Scriptures capture some of His might in these words: "The Everlasting God, the Lord, the creator of the ends of the earth, does not become weary or tired. His understanding is inscrutable. He gives strength to the weary, and to him who lacks might, he increases power."[10]

He's powerful enough to outlast time. Creative enough to bring a world of incredible variety into being. Intelligent and perceptive enough to confound the wisdom of the wise. He never runs out of energy or becomes overburdened with concerns. In fact, He gives strength and power to us who consistently run out of time, options, strength, and wisdom.

He has power to spare to make us masters of the gold sword. To have great families and strong marriages. He longs to give us this power. But only if we're willing to take a second vital step.

2. We must admit our needs and weaknesses.

Only when we kneel before the Lord and ask Him to empower us do we receive the touch of His sword on our shoulders. If we never bow our hearts, our spirits, and our wills to Him as our sovereign Lord and Master, we'll never know His power. And that's a tough thing to ask of a man who has spent a lifetime carrying his silver sword and laying it before no one.

I (John) have been watching that struggle firsthand. As I mentioned in an earlier chapter, at the time of this writing, my father lies dying in a hospital. Cancer is in a race with his failing heart to see which will end his life.

My father is a strong man. A former collegiate football player. A decorated World War II veteran. A proud man. A silver-sword expert who doesn't recognize the value or presence of a gold sword and who emotionally damaged those in two marriages and families as a result.

I've talked with him on numerous occasions about his need for the Savior. I've given him all the books I've written and anything else I thought he might read. Just recently, I gave him a tremendous new book called *Nice People Really Do Go to Hell*, by our good friend Jay Carty.[11]

I can see the war being fought in his mind and heart between bowing in faith and continuing to "walk on alone." And with the clock ticking down

If we never bow our hearts, our spirits, and our wills to Him as our sovereign Lord and Master, we'll never know His power.

to weeks or even days before his time of judgment, his knee still hasn't bent—yet.

And I know why. It's something I inherited from him and that caused me to struggle before my knee finally bent: pride. This misguided pride keeps many of us men from seeing our need of a Savior ... or of a gold sword to use with our families. And unfortunately, neither our Savior nor the gold sword looks as full of beauty and majesty unless we're on our knees in humility and faith.

We heard a story recently that captures this point extremely well. It seems that years ago, a famous sculptor was commissioned to create a statue of Christ for a large church. Bringing all his skill to bear, he crafted an image of Jesus that had people waiting in line for blocks to view it when it was unveiled. Everyone raved about this masterpiece—except a local art critic.

He went to the church midweek to view the statue when no one else was around, and he found it to be nothing out of the ordinary. The statue stood at the front of the church, and from his vantage point halfway back in the sanctuary, it looked average at best. That's just what he was going to write in his column the next day ... except for what happened next.

A janitor walked into the sanctuary and saw the critic scribbling notes. "Would you like to see the statue from the vantage point it was designed to be viewed from?" he asked. Then he took him right up in front of the now-imposing statue and had him get on his knees and look up at a masterpiece. Needless to say, the story came out much different from what the critic had intended to write just a minute before.

I (John) have tried to be that janitor with my father. I've tried every prayer, every evangelistic question, every book I know to get him down that aisle and in front of a wonderful Savior—a mighty God who carries a silver sword that would impress any old soldier and a gold sword that would challenge any saint.

But for each of us, it's a God-ordained choice. We must choose to see God's greatness, to admit our own weakness, and also to do one more thing.

3. We must wait upon the Lord.

"Those who wait for the Lord will gain new strength;
they will mount up with wings like eagles,
they will run and not get tired,
they will walk and not become weary."[12]

It's humbling to admit we can't carry our gold sword alone every day as we should. It's humbling to realize we're often insensitive and can't carry off a lifetime marriage without His help. But it's the very place God wants us to be.

I (Gary) put perhaps the most important message I'll ever write into a book called *Joy That Lasts*.[13] In it, I tell of the lowest time in my life ... that today I realize was also the high point.

Out of the ashes of disappointment, deep hurt, and even depression, God taught me the very lesson I most needed to learn. It's a lesson that has not only built my entire ministry, but has also been my greatest motivation to carry the gold sword with my wife and family.

That lesson, explained more fully in the other book, was that when I came to the end of my limited strength, God became everything I needed and more to finally have fullness of life.

For years, I had my hopes for fulfillment pinned to people, places, and even things that I thought would bring me what I wanted most—love, peace, and joy. But instead of the rest my soul longed for, I ended up experiencing near-daily bouts with fear, anger, and worry—the very emotions I had tried so hard to avoid! Only when I hit bottom did I finally realize I had been looking at the "gifts" of life as the "source" of life.

People, places, and things were never meant to give us life. God alone is the author of a fulfilling life. He fills our cups fully, and then people, places, and things become overflow. They're nice if they meet our expectations, but they're not necessary to experience love, peace, and joy.

What freedom! Finally, I was able to use my gold sword with others without expecting anything from them in return. Because I had finally fully trusted Christ, I had more quality of life than I ever could have received

People, places, and things were never meant to give us life. God alone is the author of a fulfilling life.

from another person! Now I could serve others freely, because He was already meeting my needs. I could love my wife unconditionally, because I wasn't expecting her to fulfill every expectation or to give me what only God could give. Norma is a wonderful wife. But as my friend Larry Crabb is fond of saying, any woman can be a great spouse, but she'll make a lousy god.

If we'll learn more about who God is and the power He gives us through our Savior, Jesus Christ; if we'll humble ourselves, admitting we can't carry our sword without His help; then He promises to give us the help we need—and more. He will...

"Set our feet on solid ground."[14] For ...

"He has given us new birth into a living hope through the resurrection of Jesus Christ."[15]

And further, He promises to be our "bread" ... our "living water" ... our "rear guard" ... our "shield" ... "our strength" ...our "good shepherd" ... our "counselor" ... and our "advocate."

And it's all wrapped in the promise that even when we fail, "If anyone sins, we have an advocate with the father ... Jesus Christ."[16]

"If we confess our sins, he is faithful and just and will forgive us our sins and purify us from all unrighteousness."[17]

Then there's the incredible truth that "He Himself has said, 'I will never leave you, nor forsake you.'"[18]

What a God! What a Savior! What an example to follow in carrying the gold sword, and what a King to give our lives to in serving Him and others for a lifetime!

That's our final prayer for you—that you'll discover the incredible value and power of an average man to carry the gold sword *when he places his hand in the Savior's*, and when he uses that sword to bring out the very best in his loved ones.

NOTES

CHAPTER 1
1. Gary Smalley, *If Only He Knew* (Grand Rapids, Mich.: Zondervan, 1979).

CHAPTER 2
1. To see the lasting *harm* we can do, read Exodus 34:6-7.

CHAPTER 3
1. See Judith Wallerstein, *Second Chances* (New York: Ticknor & Fields, 1989-90). An excellent book that shows the long-term damage divorce does to children.
2. Gordon Dalbey, *Healing the Masculine Soul* (Dallas: Word, 1988), p. 18.
3. See Wallerstein, *Second Chances*, and Gary Richmond, *The Divorce Decision* (Dallas: Word, 1988).
4. See Ephesians 5:25-29.
5. Ephesians 5:28-29.
6. Proverbs 27:10.

CHAPTER 4
1. Ephesians 5:25-26.
2. Ephesians 5:28.
3. Ephesians 5:22.
4. Ephesians 5:21.
5. Ephesians 5:22.
6. We want to give a special word of thanks to our much loved and appreciated pastor at Scottsdale Bible Church, Darryl DelHousaye. A scholar of note, he provided tremendously helpful insights into Ephesians 5. If you're looking for a daily devotional, see his pocket-sized treasure, *Time for Eternity* (Sisters, Ore.: Questar, 1991).
7. Song of Solomon 1:4, NASB.
8. See, for example, Matthew 22:34-40.
9. Matthew 6:21.
10. Gary Smalley and John Trent, *The Gift of Honor* (Nashville: Nelson, 1987), p. 25.
11. Philippians 4:8, NASB, emphasis added.
12. See Ephesians 5:25-27.

CHAPTER 5

1. One such group is Promise Keepers, with its national men's conference in Colorado the last weekend of every July. For more information on this powerful, inspiring event, write to Promise Keepers, P.O. Box 18376, Boulder, CO 80308, or call (303) 843-9812.
2. Gary Smalley and John Trent, *The Gift of Honor* (Nashville: Nelson, 1987).
3. Psalm 119:11, NASB, emphasis added.
4. Psalm 119:14, NASB, emphasis added.
5. Hebrews 11:1, NASB.
6. Proverbs 22:6, NASB.
7. See Gary Smalley and John Trent, *The Language of Love* (Colorado Springs, Col.: Focus on the Family, 1988, 1991), chapter 1.

CHAPTER 6

1. Ephesians 4:26, NASB.
2. Neil Clark Warren, *Make Anger Your Ally* (Nashville: Wolgemuth & Hyatt, 1990), pp. 35, 39. See chapters 8 and 9.
3. See Christopher Peterson and Lisa Bossio, *Health and Optimism* (New York: The Free Press, 1991), pp. 116-17.
4. Warren, *Make Anger Your Ally*.
5. See Paul Meier and Frank Minirth, *Happiness Is a Choice* (Grand Rapids, Mich.: Baker, 1978).
6. See Dr. Ted Kitchen's excellent book on "discipline and restoration" called *Aftershock: What to Do When Christian Leaders (and Others) Disappoint You* (Portland, Ore.: Multnomah, 1992).
7. See Luke 6:41-42.
8. See Proverbs 15:1-4.
9. Proverbs 30:8-9, paraphrased.

CHAPTER 7

1. Jo Durden-Smith and Diane deSimone, *Sex and the Brain* (New York: Warner, 1983).
2. *Ibid.*, pp. 42-46.
3. *Time*, 1-20-92.
4. 1 Thessalonians 2:11-12.
5. Colossians 3:12, 16.
6. Ephesians 4:29.
7. Proverbs 25:11-12.

CHAPTER 8

1. Matthew 16:25.
2. Proverbs 4:23.

CHAPTER 9

1. See Ephesians 5:33.

2. See 1 Peter 3:7.

3. To better understand the concept of a closed spirit, see the newly revised version of Gary's book *The Key to Your Child's Heart* (Dallas: Word, 1992).

4. Genesis 3:16.

CHAPTER 10

1. See, for example, Kevin Leman and Randy Carlson, *Unlocking the Secrets of Your Childhood Memories* (Nashville: Nelson, 1989); Rich Buhler, *Pain and Pretending* (Nashville: Nelson, 1988).

2. An excellent book we've previewed and highly recommend is Gary Rosberg's *Choosing to Love Again*, scheduled to be published by Focus on the Family in the fall of 1992.

3. See *Indians* (Alexandria, Va.: Time-Life, 1973).

4. See Gary Smalley and John Trent, *The Blessing* (Nashville:Nelson, 1986).

5. Genesis 27:26-27.

6. See Smalley and Trent, *The Blessing*, Appendix A.

CHAPTER 12

1. J.W. Pennebaker and O'Herron, *The Journal of Abnormal Psychology*, 93, pp. 473-76.

2. *Ibid.*

3. J.W. Pennebaker, Hughes and O'Herron, "The Psychophysiology of Confession," *Journal of Personality and Social Psychology*, 52, pp. 781-93.

4. G.W. Comstock and K.B. Partridge, "Church Attendance and Health," *Journal of Chronic Diseases*, 25, pp. 665-72.

5. See Hebrews 10:24-25.

6. See Paul Meier and Frank Minirth, *Happiness Is a Choice* (Grand Rapids, Mich.: Baker, 1978).

7. See Exodus 17:8-13.

8. See Deuteronomy 32:30.

9. See note 1 for chapter 5.

10. See Gary Smalley and John Trent, *The Blessing* (Nashville: Nelson, 1986), chapter 3.

11. Proverbs 16:32, NASB.

12. See Larry Crabb's book *Inside Out* (Colorado Springs, Col.: NavPress, 1988).

13. Dr. Bill Retts is one of the finest therapists we've known in the Phoenix area.

14. Genesis 2:24-25, emphasis added.

15. Proverbs 12:15.

CHAPTER 13

1. Proverbs 12:15.

2. See Richard Stuart, *Helping Couples Change* (New York: Guilford Press, 1980).

3. Gary Smalley and John Trent, *The Blessing* (Nashville: Nelson, 1986).

4. Don and Jan Frank, *When Victims Marry* (San Bernardino, Cal.: Here's Life, 1990).

5. We refer to counselors using masculine pronouns only for the sake of brevity. We realize there are many fine women counselors.

6. For more information, contact Rapha toll free at 800-383-HOPE(4673).

7. See Ruth Graham's book *Prodigals and Those Who Love Them* (Colorado Springs, Col.: Focus on the Family, 1991).

8. See Chuck and Barb Snyder, *Incompatibility: Grounds for a Great Marriage* (Sisters, Ore.: Questar, 1990).

9. 1 Thessalonians 5:14, NASB.

10. Proverbs 27:10.

11. See Gary Smalley and John Trent, *The Two Sides of Love* (Colorado Springs, Col.: Focus on the Family, 1990).

12. Ecclesiastes 4:9.

CHAPTER 14

1. Romans 7:15, 18.

2. Matthew 3:11-12.

3. Acts 1:6.

4. John 6:15.

5. Luke 4:6-7.

6. Matthew 26:53.

7. John 18:4-8, emphasis added.

8. Exodus 3:13-14.

9. See Acts 10:42.

10. Isaiah 40:27ff.

11. Jay Carty, *Nice People Really Do Go to Hell* (Portland, Ore.: Multnomah, 1992).

12. Isaiah 40:31, NASB.

13. Gary Smalley, *Joy That Lasts* (Grand Rapids, Mich.: Zondervan, 1986).

14. Psalm 40:2.

15. 1 Peter 1:3; see vv. 3-5.

16. 1 John 2:1.

17. 1 John 1:9.

18. Hebrews 13:5.

DEVELOPING A MARRIAGE AND FAMILY CONSTITUTION

The main reasons to write a personal marriage and family constitution:

1. **It brings the family into unity.** Philippians 1:27-28 states that our "enemies" perceive any unity as a sign of destruction to themselves. Also, a house divided against itself cannot stand. Two united are stronger than one. The Lord's will is for all His children to walk in oneness (Phil. 2:2).

2. **It follows the pattern of Christ and His church.** Ephesians 5:23 explains that husbands and wives are to live by His example with the church. Headship and submission are both military terms. Desert Storm was an example of military leaders doing battle with a clearly understood plan.

3. **It reduces prolonged or angry arguments.** One form of a constitution is to agree to list all the negative and positive reasons to follow a certain course of action. Seeing the two sides of an issue can bring about quicker resolution to important decisions, and this, in turn, brings about the desired unity.

4. **It forces meaningful and honorable communication.** When members of a family agree to live in oneness, the end result is many hours of discussion in order to resolve important issues.

5. **It provides greater security and stability for each family member.** Also, the children do not experience as many unsettling surprises in discipline.

6. **It provides continual reminders of a family's most important values and rules.** The constitution is usually displayed in a prominent household location. It usually takes about 30 days to break a habit or start a new one if we are regularly working on the habit.

7. **It allows a family to prioritize its most important values.** Good things are often the enemy of the very best.

8. **A written constitution can become the policing force at home.** This then allows each member of a family to show greater love and comfort whenever an article of the constitution is violated.

9. **It can reduce stress and bring greater relaxation.** Each member of a family knows that the other members are aware of each other's needs and important concerns.

10. **The Lord's contract with His children is that He will never leave them or forsake them,** and He promises to meet their needs through His riches in glory (Phil. 4:19). "For God so loved the world. . ." (John 3:16).

TEN POSSIBLE ARTICLES OF A FAMILY CONSTITUTION

1. We recognize that God loves us and will meet all our needs through His riches in glory. We also realize He will use our trials to bless us and develop more of His love within us.
2. We purpose this day to honor God and His creation above ourselves.
3. We agree to resolve any angry conflicts between ourselves each day before the sun sets.
4. We resolve this day to lovingly and meaningfully touch each other as needed on a daily basis.
5. We understand the value of spending meaningful time together. Therefore, we agree to schedule regular monthly activities that each family member can enthusiastically support.
6. We recognize that all our money belongs to the Lord, and we purpose to seek His will and wisdom regarding the earning, giving, saving, and any other use of His funds.
7. We further recognize that God has created each person as a unique individual with differing strengths and personality characteristics. Therefore, we will endeavor to discover these differences and learn to accept and praise them.
8. We each recognize the great importance of daily meaningful communication between one another. Therefore, we purpose to spend the necessary time each day, as possible, to carefully listen to each other and to express our deepest thoughts and needs.
9. We resolve to care for one another in a tender and affectionate manner.
10. We agree to believe the best in each other and to trust the words and actions of one another as honest. If this trust is broken at any time, we all agree to restore the trust by confessing the untruths, by seeking forgiveness, and by making any necessary restitution.

A Model
Family Constitution
Developed at
SBC Men's Retreat

With the help of the men of Scottsdale Bible Church in Scottsdale, Arizona, the following "Gold Sword" goals for family constitutions were developed as a model. These are summary challenges for each man in our church to adopt as his own, to God's glory and for the betterment of our families.

HONOR:

We honor God above all by submitting to the authority of His Word in all things. This honor must extend to our families first, and then to others. We must honor God's creations and those He has put in positions of authority. Traits of this honor are obedience, understanding, respect, responsibility, praise, and, above all, love. We will show honor by how we treat others, possessions, and God's creation, thinking more highly of others than of ourselves.

PERSONALITY STRENGTHS:

Realizing that our differences were a major factor in our being drawn together as husbands and wives, we will seek always to keep that "first love" commitment alive by valuing our differences. Additionally, we will actively seek to understand more about the other person's viewpoint, thought process, and natural reactions as a way of increasing our understanding and appreciation. Taking seriously the admonition that we are not all an "eye, or an ear" but different yet important parts of God's body, we will seek to value all members of our households and live with them in an understanding way.

ANGER:

In our families, we purpose to shut out unhealthy anger with each other. When we talk about issues, we will be slow to speak, quick to listen, and slow to anger (James 1:19). When anger occurs, we will recognize the individual differences among us, but we will not allow the sun to go down on our anger (Eph. 4:26). We will strive to identify the causes of the anger and deal with those causes instead of ignoring them. And without exception, if we cross the line into unhealthy anger with our tone of voice, words, or actions, we will seek the forgiveness of those we have hurt (Matt. 18:22).

MEANINGFUL TOUCH:

We agree to provide every family member with abundant praise and encouragement, combined with affectionate touch. This may include hugs, holding hands, or other loving expressions agreed on by the couple. We pledge to do this consistently, even when our feelings may be in conflict.

COMMUNICATION:

We pledge to take the time to speak regularly about those things that are important to us and our loved ones. We will take seriously their frustrations, fears, disappointments, burdens, and dreams.

We further pledge to seek actively to communicate our love verbally. We will do this daily. Additionally, we will carve out the communication time our spouses need so that we might find unity, intimacy, and peace in our relationships, that God might be honored.

FAMILY BONDING EXPERIENCES:

Because we are called to "number our days," we make a commitment to measure out meaningful time with our wives and children. We will seek to provide consistent family bonding activities that are not based on money spent, but on time spent together. To do so, we will sit down as a family and find out each person's needs and likes, and then we will develop as many activities as we can that provide a warm, family experience.

FINANCES:

We pledge to communicate the financial needs of our families. We will set goals to establish a budget in order to free ourselves from the bondage of poor money management. We promise to limit the use of credit cards and to never use money as a means of controlling our families. Our resources are to be shared in an honoring way and used to further the gospel of Christ.